Damascus

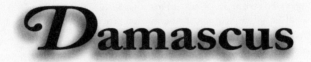

Damascus

by LUCY HECKMAN

THOROUGHBRED
Legends®

No. 22

EP

ECLIPSE
PRESS

Lexington, Kentucky

Library of Congress Control Number: 2003112333

ISBN 1-58150-111-0

Printed in The United States
First Edition: January 2004

Distributed to the trade by
National Book Network
4720-A Boston Way
Lanham, MD 20706
1.800.462.6420

a division of
Blood-Horse Publications
PUBLISHERS SINCE 1916

DAMASCUS

CONTENTS

DAMASCUS

INTRODUCTION

A Golden Age

The sixties were a true golden age of racing. These were the days before the Breeders' Cup, when top purses were $100,000 and not $1 million; the Jockey Club Gold Cup was still run at two miles; and great horses could withstand the rigors of racing every week instead of every month. This was a time when those who could not get to the track could watch Win Elliot's *Race of the Week* on their black-and-white television sets and listen to the thrilling stretch calls of legendary announcers such as Fred Caposella. Also, then, like now, race fans were hungry for a Triple Crown winner, given the drought since Citation won in 1948.

In 1967 Edith Bancroft's Damascus almost quenched race fans' thirst for a Triple Crown winner after taking two of the three classics. The compact bay colt came along on the heels of Kelso, the charismatic gelding who dominated the early sixties, earning Horse of the Year titles five times.

Following Kelso's reign, Damascus kept race goers and television viewers on the edge of their seats with his patented stretch run that left the competition struggling in his wake. Guided by the great trainer Frank Whiteley Jr. and piloted in most of his races by the renowned Bill Shoemaker, the three-year-old Damascus swept the country in 1967, winning races at Arlington Park, Saratoga, Aqueduct, and Delaware Park.

Two other outstanding horses that captivated the public around the same time were the 1966 three-year-old champion and Horse of the Year Buckpasser and the lightning-fast Dr. Fager, from the same crop as Damascus. The "Big Three" of racing crossed swords in the Woodward Stakes on September 30, 1967, at Aqueduct. An overflowing crowd of 55,259 watched as Damascus won by an astonishing ten lengths. The distinction led him to be named Horse of the Year over his two fabled rivals — a truly brilliant and amazing achievement.

During his Horse of the Year season, Damascus won just about every major race for three year olds save one (the Kentucky Derby), inspiring Tom Ainslie to write: "the Damascus of the Summer of 1967 was a horse for the ages."

Charles Hatton perhaps best summarized Damascus' running style in the 1968 *American Racing Manual*:

"It was thrilling to see him fighting back, eyes blazing, lengthening his stride so that his neck and tail were on a straight line, in a heated debate the last frenetic yards. He was the archetype of the throatlatcher who is reluctant to leave his opposition. Usually he had put all rivals on a treadmill in the early stretch, but when circumstances conspired to place him on his mettle he was courage itself."

Damascus achieved his greatness in his penultimate year of racing, but his rivalry with Dr. Fager continued into their four-year-old season, for which Dr. Fager was awarded his own Horse of the Year title.

The debate about Damascus versus Dr. Fager raged among fans, and excitement built in anticipation of each of their four match-ups. Damascus and Dr. Fager formed one of the greatest rivalries in racing history, right up there with Nashua and Swaps; Sunday Silence and Easy Goer; and Affirmed and Alydar. Electricity was in the air when these horses matched strides down the stretch. At the end of their careers Damascus and Dr. Fager had each notched two victories over the other. Even though the races were more than forty years ago, veteran race goers still argue about their memorable duels.

Damascus' status as a racing legend is undisputed. His impressive race record makes it impossible to forget the images of the compact bay colt that came from out of nowhere to sweep by rivals in the stretch, with each stride increasing his margin of victory.

Lucy Heckman
Queens Village, New York, August 2003

DAMASCUS

CHAPTER 1

Mrs. Bancroft's Racing Stable

When Damascus entered the world on April 14, 1964, at John A. Bell III's Jonabell Farm near Lexington, Kentucky, he became part of a long-standing heritage that had begun in the early 1900s with William Woodward Sr.'s inheritance of Belair Stud.

The bay colt by Sword Dancer—Kerala, by My Babu, was one of a few horses owned and bred by Woodward's daughter Edith Woodward Bancroft. Damascus' jockeys would wear the Woodward family's famous white silks with red polka dots and scarlet cap that the Belair Stud's past greats had carried to victory. These included America's only father and son Triple Crown winners Gallant Fox and Omaha, as well as dual classic winner Nashua, whose bid to join his illustrious Belair predecessors as a member of the Triple Crown elite was foiled at the outset, when the upstart from the West, Swaps, defeated him in the 1955 Kentucky Derby. Time would tell how well the youngster would live up to the reputations of the earlier Belair colorbearers.

Bancroft, the eldest of the Woodward children, was continuing a family tradition embraced by her father and all too briefly continued by her ill-fated brother William Woodward Jr.

William Woodward Sr. was born in 1876 and educated at Groton and Harvard. Woodward Sr.'s first job after receiving his degree from Harvard Law School was secretary to Joseph Choate, the U.S. ambassador to the Court of St. James in England. The time in England helped fuel Woodward Sr.'s keen interest in horse racing, and he often attended races at courses such as Ascot, Epsom, and Newmarket with none other than King Edward VII, who owned and bred horses, including 1896 English Derby winner Persimmon and 1900 English Triple Crown winner Diamond Jubilee. Woodward Sr. had become a part of King Edward's inner circle and shared the monarch's devotion to the spectacle and pageantry of racing. Seeing Volodyovski, a colt owned by American financier W.C. Whitney, win the English Derby in 1901 stirred in Woodward Sr. a lifelong dream to win this race with a horse that he bred and owned.

Returning to New York circa 1903, Woodward Sr. became vice president of Hanover National Bank. Soon after his return, he met the young woman who would become his wife, Elsie Cryder, daughter of the successful businessman Duncan Cryder. Elsie, whose given name was Elizabeth, was a triplet, and she and her siblings, Ethel and Edith, were born in 1882.

In 1891 the girls' uncle, W. Wetmore Cryder, was indicted for perjury and embezzling $39,000 from Manhattan Square Bank, where he was president. The family scandal prompted Duncan Cryder to take his family to Paris. There Elsie and her siblings lived what she later called a "life of leisure." The triplets were educated by their governesses and toured Europe with their parents. In 1899 the triplets, now lovely young socialites, and their parents returned to New York. The Cryder triplets' comings and goings at dinners, parties, and other events regularly made the society columns. Their striking good looks inspired "Gibson Girl" artist Charles Dana Gibson to sketch them — the ultimate accolade for young ladies of society.

In 1903 Elsie Cryder met the young banker William Woodward Sr., and after a courtship that included visits to Saratoga Race Course, the two were married on October 24, 1904, in one of the major social events of the season.

Six years after the wedding William Woodward Sr. became heir to a banking fortune when his uncle James Woodward passed away. Along with a controlling interest in Hanover National Bank in New York, Woodward Sr. inherited his uncle's Maryland horse farm, Belair Stud, in Bowie, Maryland. Established circa 1742, Belair had the distinction of being the oldest continuously operated farm in America.

Woodward Sr.'s uncle had purchased the historic property in 1898 with an eye toward his nephew's growing interest in racing. But Thoroughbreds were nothing new to Belair. About 1737, long before the state of Maryland was even a consideration, her provincial governor, Samuel Ogle, and a partner, Benjamin Tasker, began acquiring the land that would become Belair. Ogle later purchased Tasker's interest and then married his former partner's daughter. In 1742 the newlyweds left for England. Upon their return five years later, the Ogles brought back a gift from Lord Baltimore, the English proprietor of the Maryland colony: two Thoroughbreds that traced to the Royal Stud. With his English education in the sport of racing duly ingrained, Ogle began breeding and racing horses in the colony. His enthusiastic involvement led to the establishment of the Maryland Jockey Club.

In the mid-1700s Belair was home to the great racehorse and broodmare Selima, an ancestress of sixteen-time leading sire Lexington, who had such a profound influence on the modern breed.

As the Ogle family's fortunes waned, especially during the Civil War, Belair's luster faded until the Woodward family rescued and restored the farm.

William Woodward Sr. bred his first stakes winner, Lion d'Or, at Belair in 1916. Woodward Sr.'s aim was to breed Thoroughbreds capable of running classic distances. Soon the white silks with red polka dots frequently graced the racetracks of both Europe and the United States. Woodward Sr. subsequently bred more than ninety stakes winners in the United States and Europe, including Gallant Fox and Omaha, Flambette, Petee-Wrack, Flares, Vagrancy, Black Tarquin, and

Apache. Woodward Sr. purchased and raced Johnstown, the 1939 Kentucky Derby winner, who went on to be the maternal grandsire of the last great horse he bred, Nashua.

Woodward Sr.'s early dreams of success as an owner-breeder were realized in his lifetime. He was elected to The Jockey Club in 1917 and from 1930 to 1950 served as its chairman. Woodward Sr. referred to himself as a Victorian. He dressed, spoke, and behaved accordingly, by displaying reserve, dignity, and conservatism. Though a traditionalist, he accepted changes. For instance, he agreed to support the introduction of pari-mutuel betting in New York in 1940 but only if admission fees were raised to discourage those who could not afford to gamble. The one dream that Woodward Sr. did not achieve was breeding and owning a winner of the English Derby, although he came close with Prince Simon who finished second in 1950.

Elsie Woodward, who became a leading society hostess, shared her husband's interest in racing. Mrs. Woodward was regarded as a perfect hostess and also a tireless worker on behalf of hospitals and other causes. During World War I, Elsie Woodward aided in the war effort by helping servicemen at Fort Adams in Newport, Rhode Island, learn French to prepare for their arrival abroad.

In addition to Edith, nicknamed Edie, the Woodward children were Elizabeth, Sarah, Ethel, and William Jr. Of all the children, Edith Woodward demonstrated the most interest in Thoroughbred racing. She accompanied her father to the races in the United States and Europe and learned about his horses and their pedigrees. She attended the exclusive Foxcroft School in Virginia, and on June 12, 1929, she married Princeton graduate and businessman Thomas Bancroft in an elegant society wedding.

Thomas Bancroft was a textile executive and chairman of the Mount Vernon Mills of Baltimore. The Bancrofts had two sons, Thomas Jr. and William, who regularly accompanied their mother and grandmother to the races.

In 1953 William Woodward Sr. passed away, and his son inherited Belair. Among the horses William Woodward Jr. inherited was future Horse of the Year Nashua, a 1952 colt by Nasrullah—Segula, by Johnstown. The younger Woodward and trainer James

"Sunny Jim" Fitzsimmons, the stable's longtime trainer, campaigned their great Nashua to victories that included the Preakness, Belmont, and the famous match race with Kentucky Derby winner Swaps.

Imbued with her father's love of racing, Edith Bancroft kept one horse from his estate, Lucrece, a daughter of one of her favorites of her father's stakes winners, the English champion Black Tarquin. Lucrece would produce the first winner for Edith.

William Woodward Jr.'s life came to a tragic end in October 1955 when his wife, Ann, allegedly thinking he was a prowler, shot and killed him in their Long Island home. A grand jury found that no crime had been committed. The Woodward stable, including eventual 1955 Horse of the Year Nashua, was subsequently dispersed. Nashua became the first horse to sell for more than $1 million when a syndicate headed by Kentucky horseman Leslie Combs II made the successful bid.

Edith Bancroft and her mother, however, inherited the famed Belair colors, although they did not use Belair as a stable name. Mrs. Bancroft raced in her own name, though her mother was quite an active participant. On March 30, 1959, the *New York Times* heralded the return of the Belair silks to racing when Mrs. Bancroft's two-year-old colt Quadreme, a son of Greek Ship and Lucrece, set foot that day on Jamaica Race Course in the sixth race. The article noted that the silks had not been seen at Jamaica since October 28, 1955, when First Flower finished third in a race there. On July 28, 1959, Quadreme became Mrs. Bancroft's first winner with a victory at Jamaica.

Mrs. Bancroft and her mother had started serious work on building a stable, using Claiborne Farm owner A.B. Hancock Jr. as an adviser and Sunny Jim Fitzsimmons as a trainer. Hancock purchased three fillies on their behalf: Kerala, by My Babu—Blade of Time; Cycle, by Cyclotron—Vashti; and Crème Brulee, by Double Jay—Desert Sun II. Kerala was acquired for $9,600 from Duval A. Headley, who consigned her for breeder Greentree Stud to the 1959 Keeneland summer yearling sale. Mrs. Bancroft later would purchase a fourth filly, Penny Bryn, by Tulyar—Grey Streak.

Fitzsimmons took the fillies to train but advised they would make better breeding stock. The fillies thus went to their new and permanent home, Jonabell Farm, where Edith Bancroft boarded her horses.

Kerala's first two foals were both fillies: the winner Full View (1962), by Nadir, and the stakes-placed Aunt Tilt (1963), by Tulyar. The next stallion to whom Kerala would be bred was the 1959 Horse of the Year Sword Dancer, owned by Mrs. Bancroft's friend Isabel Dodge Sloane, mistress of Brookmeade Stable. The handsome blaze-faced chestnut had had an outstanding racing career before being retired to stud in 1960.

This mating was not without due consideration. According to Bennett "Benny" Bell Williams, daughter of Jonabell owner John A. Bell III, "Kerala was very high-strung, which was one of the reasons to send her to Sword Dancer as he was level-headed."

Sword Dancer, who stood at Darby Dan Farm near Lexington, presented Kerala's foal with another legacy besides an even disposition — a genetic link to a fragile sire line. Sword Dancer's great-great grandsire Teddy was the head of a line of stallions that dominated racing during the thirties and forties. The line was diminishing in influence in the fifties and early sixties, and Horse of the Year Sword Dancer offered some hope for its revival. Kerala's son Damascus bore the continuation of that hope.

CHAPTER 2

The Teddy Line

Damascus closely resembled his dam's side of the family. Instead of inheriting the bright chestnut color or the blaze and three stockings of his sire, Sword Dancer, Damascus was a bay like his dam, Kerala, and had a small white star on his forehead and a white marking around the right rear ankle almost identical to that of his maternal grandsire, My Babu. Damascus' most striking feature were his eyes — the color of vivid amber.

Sword Dancer was, at the time of Damascus' foaling, an unproven sire, but he had a formidable race record and a pedigree that combined American and European bloodlines. Most significantly, Sword Dancer was a scion of the Teddy male line, something he had in common with Triple Crown winners Gallant Fox, Omaha, and Citation. Therefore, Sword Dancer's legacy to

Damascus included not only racing talent but also the genes of one of the twentieth century's outstanding sires and sire of sires.

The story of Damascus' illustrious ancestor Teddy began in France in 1913 when Teddy, a colt by Ajax from Rondeau, was foaled. Bred by Edmond Blanc, a leading owner and breeder in France, Teddy was sold as a yearling to Captain Jefferson Davis Cohn. Since Teddy's then fourteen-year-old dam had not yet produced a winner, Cohn purchased Teddy for the relatively modest price of 5,400 francs (one thousand dollars). Named after his godfather Jefferson Davis, president of the Confederate States of America, Cohn was a prominent businessman in Great Britain and France. He was a majority shareholder of the Compagnie Internationale des Wagons Lits of France and contributed to the early development of the travel company Thomas Cook of England. He became the toast of European society and made headlines in 1922 when he purchased the Maria Theresa necklace for a reported 200,000 British pounds. Reportedly sold to finance the purchase of an airplane that could be used to stage a coup d'etat in Austria-Hungary by former emperor

Charles, the necklace had belonged to Austrian empress Maria Theresa, the mother of the doomed French queen Marie Antoinette.

Cohn started young in horse racing, owning his first winner at age fourteen. At the time of his purchase of Teddy, Cohn was a leading owner of racehorses in France.

The outbreak of World War I in 1914 interrupted racing in Europe and, consequently, Teddy was unraced at two. Racing resumed in Spain in 1916, and Cohn entered Teddy in the prestigious Grand Prix of San Sebastian, which the colt won convincingly. Teddy went on to race in both Spain and France and became a stakes winner at three and four, winning the St. Leger de San Sebastian, Prix des Trois Ans, Prix de Darney, and the Prix des Sablonnieres. At the end of Teddy's career, Cohn's colt had won six of eight starts and earned 145,000 francs (approximately $26,000).

Sent to stud in France in 1918, Teddy achieved immediate success. His most successful performers were Ortello, winner of the Prix de l'Arc de Triomphe; Rose of England, winner of the English Oaks; Asterus, winner of the Champion Stakes; and Sir Gallahad III, winner of the Poule d'Essai des Poulains (French Two Thousand Guineas) and later an influential American sire.

Sir Gallahad III, Teddy's son from Plucky Liege, was imported in 1926 to A.B. Hancock Sr.'s Claiborne Farm in Kentucky, where he would have a tremendous impact as a sire. His first crop included Woodward Sr.'s 1930 Triple Crown winner Gallant Fox, who, in turn, sired 1935 Triple Crown winner Omaha. Among his other best offspring were Kentucky Derby winners Gallahadion and Hoop, Jr. and Woodward Sr.'s champion filly Vagrancy. This sire line did not flourish after the early 1940s, and except for a brief return through Sir Gallahad III's stakes-winning son Roman, it faded into obscurity. However, Sir Gallahad III proved to be a valuable broodmare sire and led the list twelve years, ten times consecutively. He remains a viable part of the female line in many modern pedigrees.

Bull Dog, a stakes-winning full brother to Sir Gallahad III, came to the United States in 1930 and, like his sibling, achieved immediate success, topping the sire list in 1943 and the broodmare sire list for three years. His most influential son was, without a doubt, Bull Lea, leading U.S. sire for five years and leading broodmare sire for four. Bull Lea's offspring made the famed Calumet Farm an unqualified success throughout the 1940s and 1950s. Among Bull Lea's offspring were the great Citation, 1948 Triple Crown winner; Horse of the Year and champion mare Twilight Tear; Kentucky Derby winners Iron Liege and Hill Gail; Horse of the Year and handicap star Armed; and champions Coaltown, Real Delight, and Bewitch. Unfortunately, Bull Lea's sons did not replicate their sire's influence, and this male line went into a decline. Perhaps the most disappointing of Bull Lea's sons at stud was Citation, who did produce a champion filly in Silver Spoon and a Preakness winner in Fabius but was only average as a sire. Furthermore, Citation's sons did nothing to revitalize the male line and, thus, the Bull Dog branch tailed off.

Teddy's imported daughter, La Troienne, would have a most significant impact on the female lines of American racehorses for decades. La Troienne was purchased in December 1930 by Colonel E.R. Bradley who sent her to his Idle Hour Stock Farm in Kentucky. La Troienne became the dam of champions Black Helen and Bimelech, and her descendants included Busanda, Buckpasser, Affectionately, Personality, Numbered Account, Busher, Relaxing, and Easy Goer.

Teddy stood in France for most of his stud career, but the 1929 stock market crash changed his life and impacted American racing. Cohn lost his money in the crash, necessitating the sale of Teddy, in 1931, to F. Wallis Armstrong, owner of Meadowview Farm, and Kenneth N. Gilpin, owner of Kentmere Farm and, later, president of the Fasig-Tipton Sales Company. Teddy arrived in the United States on July 28, 1931, and began stud duty at Kentmere Farm in Virginia in 1932 for a fee of $2,500. Teddy became a much sought-after and popular stallion in the United States until his death from a twisted intestine in 1936.

On the racetrack most of Teddy's American offspring did not measure up to his European progeny. His best American offspring were Case Ace and Sun Teddy. Case Ace, a stakes winner, had some success as a sire, and his best foal was Belmont Stakes winner Pavot. However, like so many of the other males of this line, Pavot did not turn out to be a successful sire. Case Ace carried on the broodmare sire tradition of the Teddy line, and his name appears in the pedigrees of champions and leading sires, thanks to his stakes-winning daughter, Raise You. When bred to Native Dancer, Raise You produced the champion and immensely successful stallion Raise a Native, who sired classic winner Majestic Prince, stakes winner and leading sire Alydar, and Mr. Prospector, one of the most celebrated and notable sires in racing history. Raise a Native's sons sired, among others, Horse of the Year Alysheba, Triple Crown winner Affirmed, and classic winners Coastal, Genuine Risk, Easy Goer, and Fusaichi Pegasus.

It was Sun Teddy, a chestnut son of Teddy out of Sunmelia foaled in 1933, who was fated to carry on the male line. Calumet Farm purchased Sun Teddy as a yearling, and he did well on the racetrack, winning eight of eighteen starts and scoring victories in the Arlington and Saranac handicaps. Sun Teddy entered stud in 1938, and that season he was bred to the Calumet mare Hug Again, resulting in a foal named Sun Again.

A striking chestnut colt with a blaze, Sun Again performed well for Calumet, winning the Arlington Futurity and the Dixie, Equipoise Mile, and McLennan handicaps. Called by the *New York Times* the "Calumet Meteor," he defeated his stablemate, 1941 Triple Crown winner Whirlaway, as well as 1942 Kentucky Derby victor Shut Out. Other good stakes performers by Sun Teddy included Air Patrol ($163,100) and Sun Herod ($162,045).

Retired to Calumet, where he stood for a respectable fee of $2,500, Sun Again greatly improved upon Sun Teddy, who sired only six stakes winners. Sun Again's thirty stakes-winning colts and fillies included Calumet's champion three-year-old filly Wistful; champion sprinter White Skies; and successful handicap performers Palestinian and Sunglow.

Sunglow, who inherited his sire's blazed face and chestnut coat, was a foal of 1947 out of the Mad Hatter mare Rosern, a daughter of English Oaks winner Rosedrop and a half sister to 1918 English Triple Crown winner and leading English sire Gainsborough.

Most accounts of Mad Hatter indicate that the colt lived up to his name although the fiery son of Fair Play was an outstanding handicap horse, winning such important races as the Metropolitan Handicap and the Jockey Club Gold Cup.

Isabel Dodge Sloane's Brookmeade Stable owned Sunglow, and the colt was an able and durable performer, winning nine of forty-five races. At the time Sunglow raced, Mrs. Sloane, daughter of one of the Dodge brothers of the automobile company fame, was a leading owner and had won the 1934 Kentucky Derby with Cavalcade. A successful breeder in her own right, Sloane was also an astute buyer of racing stock and often attended the sales, looking for additions to her racing stable. In 1948 at the Keeneland sales, a strong, well-balanced chestnut colt bred and consigned by Walter J. Salmon's Mereworth Farm caught her eye, and she was high bidder at eight thousand dollars. Among his six stakes victories, Sunglow won the Discovery Handicap, setting a track record for one and one-eighth miles, and the Widener Handicap. He retired to stud at Mereworth Farm in Kentucky with earnings of $168,275 but did not duplicate the success of his sire nor get great numbers of foals. He did, however, beget one son who not only inherited the color and the markings of his sire and grandsire but also resurrected the classic abilities of his ancestors.

Mrs. Sloane bred and raced Sword Dancer, a 1956

colt by Sunglow from Highland Fling. Sword Dancer
was a muscular but smallish chestnut colt, about 15.3
hands, with a blazed face and three white stockings.
His dam Highland Fling did not race because of a split
pastern but was by 1944 champion three-year-old colt
By Jimminy out of the Royal Minstrel mare Swing
Time, a daughter of War Relic's full sister, Speed Boat
(by Man o' War). Speed Boat had also produced 1940
champion two-year-old filly Level Best, by Equipoise.
Highland Fling, in an interesting footnote, was the
source of a huge profit. Brookmeade sold her for two
thousand dollars in 1957 when Sword Dancer was a
yearling. In 1959, when Sword Dancer became Horse
of the Year, her owner, Philip Godfrey, who had also
campaigned Highland Fling's stakes-winning half sister
O'Alison, sold her for $80,000 to Mrs. E.H. Augustus,
owner of Keswick Stable in Virginia.

Hall of Fame trainer Elliott Burch, who later developed such standouts as Arts and Letters and Fort
Marcy, trained Sword Dancer. Sword Dancer was a late
developer, taking eight starts as a two-year-old to win
a maiden race in the latter part of 1958. That year he
also won the Mayflower Stakes and subsequently fin-

ished third to First Landing in the Garden State Stakes and fourth in the Remsen Stakes. At the end of 1958, Sword Dancer was given a respectable 122 pounds on the Experimental Free Handicap for two-year-olds, compared to champion First Landing's highweight of 128 pounds.

Brookmeade and Elliott Burch began Sword Dancer's three-year-old campaign in the winter of 1959 at Gulfstream Park. In his first start at three, the colt finished fifth in the Hutcheson Stakes, which was won by Easy Spur. Gradually rounding to form, Sword Dancer won an allowance race and then finished second to Easy Spur in the Florida Derby. Sword Dancer rebounded to win the Stepping Stone Purse, this time defeating Easy Spur, and became one of the horses to watch in the Kentucky Derby. However, it was Tomy Lee who won the Kentucky Derby over Sword Dancer in a memorable stretch duel. As Sword Dancer moved ahead at the stretch turn, Bill Shoemaker, riding Tomy Lee, thought that Bill Boland was going to win with Sword Dancer and shouted to Boland: "Good luck. I hope you win it." But Tomy Lee had something left and caught Sword Dancer at the wire, winning by a nose. Tomy Lee, running to the inside of Sword Dancer, had drifted out in the stretch, causing Boland to object, a claim that the stewards disallowed.

Tomy Lee's trainer, Frank Childs, opted out of the Preakness, and Shoemaker rode Sword Dancer instead. Royal Orbit, however, was much the best that day, defeating Sword Dancer by four lengths. Tuning up for the Belmont Stakes, Sword Dancer won the mile Metropolitan Handicap against older horses under Shoemaker, who returned to ride Sword Dancer in his next three starts. In the Belmont, Sword Dancer came from fifteen lengths off the pace to defeat Bagdad, with Royal Orbit finishing third.

Sword Dancer won his next start, the Monmouth Handicap, then finished second in a very dramatic Brooklyn Handicap. Nervous and edgy before the race, he crashed through the starting gate, running a six-teenth of a mile before being brought back; then despite swerving at the start, he finished a game second to Babu (no relation to My Babu). Sword Dancer then went on to annex the Travers Stakes at Saratoga. Manuel Ycaza, who rode the Sunglow colt in the Travers, was quoted by *New York Times* reporter Joe

Nichols: "(Sword Dancer)'s small in size but big in heart. He gives you absolutely everything he has."

To win Horse of the Year honors, Sword Dancer needed to defeat his main rivals, 1958 Horse of the Year Round Table and the outstanding stakes winner Hillsdale. The crucible for these powerful forces would be 1959's "race of the year," the Woodward Stakes. Ridden by Eddie Arcaro in the Woodward, Sword Dancer outdueled Hillsdale in the stretch, with Round Table finishing third. Sword Dancer clinched Horse of the Year honors by defeating Round Table in the Jockey Club Gold Cup. He completed his three-year-old campaign with earnings of $537,004.

The disposition and appearance of three-year-old Sword Dancer were described by Charles Hatton in the 1960 *American Racing Manual*: "...Sword Dancer as he appears to one observer to say he is a bright chestnut, light and airy of frame, his demeanor eager and full of joie de vivre. His vivacity, particularly in the walking ring for the Woodward and the Jockey Club Gold Cup, delighted blasé habitués of the paddocks...Sword Dancer's head and the set of his ears come to rather a plain frontispiece, relieved by a spectacular blaze and a luminous sociable eye."

Unfortunately, Sword Dancer's four-year-old campaign was not nearly as grand as that of his sophomore year. For William H. Rudy's book *Racing in America, 1960–1979*, trainer Elliott Burch commented: "The trouble with his four-year-old campaign was his glorious reputation — which put the weight on him. His limit was 126 pounds. When he got more than that, he lost." Sword Dancer did win the Grey Lag and Suburban handicaps and another Woodward Stakes. He suffered a career-ending injury during a workout on November 6, 1960, and was retired to stud at Darby Dan Farm. He ended his career with fifteen wins in thirty-nine starts and earnings of $829,610. Seventeen years later Sword Dancer would be elected to the Racing Hall of Fame.

One of the mares presented to Sword Dancer in his third year at stud was Edith Bancroft's unraced mare, Kerala, a daughter of My Babu and Blade of Time. Her pedigree complemented that of Sword Dancer, offering a fairly solid background and an already proven link to the all-important Teddy.

Kerala's dam, the unraced Blade of Time, was by the imported Sickle out of Bar Nothing, a half sister to

1926 Kentucky Derby winner Bubbling Over. To the cover of La Troienne's son Bimelech, Blade of Time had already produced the stakes winners Bymeabond, Blue Border, and Guillotine. Thus, the highly desirable Sword Dancer would be a likely choice for a daughter of Blade of Time since he offered a direct genetic link with the prepotent Teddy. In addition to the nick with Teddy, mating Blade of Time's daughter to Sword Dancer provided inbreeding to two formidable names in pedigrees: Phalaris and Blue Larkspur.

Blade of Time's sire Sickle was a son of Phalaris, a cornerstone of the modern breed. Her dam, Bar Nothing, was a daughter of champion and Hall of Famer Blue Larkspur. By Jimminy, the sire of Sword Dancer's dam Highland Fling, was by Pharamond II, a full brother to Sickle, out of the Blue Larkspur mare Buginarug.

Blue Larkspur was a homebred for Col. Bradley, who considered the colt to be his greatest horse as well as one of his personal favorites. Blue Larkspur won ten of sixteen starts, and his stakes victories included the Juvenile Stakes, Saratoga Special, Belmont Stakes, Withers Stakes, and the Stars and Stripes Handicap. He was a successful sire and broodmare sire and among his outstanding offspring were Blue Swords, Revoked, Myrtlewood, and Blue Delight.

As products of the Bradley breeding program, Blue Larkspur and his granddaughter Blade of Time were given names beginning with the traditional "Bradley B." Superstitious by nature, Bradley thought giving his horses names starting with the letter B would be lucky and indeed it was in many cases, such as with his Kentucky Derby winners Behave Yourself, Bubbling Over, Burgoo King, and Brokers Tip.

Kerala's sire My Babu had been imported to the United States in 1956. An attractive bay son of Djebel, My Babu was foaled in 1945 in France and raced in England for his owner, the Maharajah Gaekwar of Baroda in India.

Champion two-year-old colt in England in 1947, My Babu at three won a classic, the Two Thousand Guineas, and the Craven Stakes; at four he won the Victoria Cup. He was sent to stud with an outstanding racing record and pedigree. His sire, Djebel, was a leading sire in France and his dam, the unraced Perfume II, was a half sister to outstanding American sire Ambiorix and to Source Sucree, the dam of leading sire Turn-to. Doing well at stud in Europe, My Babu was syndicated for a reported $600,000 in 1955 to stand at Spendthrift Farm and was flown to Kentucky on July 9, 1956, from Shannon Airport in Ireland, the first horse ever to make a direct flight from Europe to Kentucky. The pilot of that plane, Nick Lutz, was quoted by *The Blood-Horse*: "That horse sure is a gentleman. He weathered a storm outside of New York better than a lot of humans would. He slipped down a couple of times but he got right up and didn't raise a fuss." The gentlemanliness of My Babu would be a trait handed down to his grandson, Damascus. My Babu excelled as a sire and as a broodmare sire. His stakes-winning offspring included Crozier, Our Babu, and Gambetta. In addition to Damascus, My Babu would be the broodmare sire of champions Gamely and Little Current.

At the comparatively advanced age of nineteen, Blade of Time was bred to the even-tempered My Babu, standing his first American season at stud in 1957, and they produced Kerala, her final foal.

Regarding Blade of Time's pedigree, Charles Hatton commented in the 1968 *American Racing Manual*:

"Some of the Sickles were hot under the collar, as Andrew Jackson Joyner used to say, declaring: 'I wouldn't ride one of them as a gift.' Joseph E. Widener had numerous Sickle fillies who were so obstreperous at the gate, they never raced."

Regardless of her temperamental relatives, Blade of Time turned out to be a broodmare of the highest quality and in addition to the aforementioned stakes winners produced an additional stakes winner in Ruddy.

My Babu provided an outcross for Blade of Time, and his gentleness perhaps balanced some of the obstreperousness of the Sickle blood in her pedigree.

Whatever the inner workings that took place in the spin of the genetic wheel when Kerala conceived to Sword Dancer, the resulting foal, named Damascus, carved his own significant niche in the history of the Thoroughbred.

DAMASCUS

CHAPTER 3

A Promising Colt

As a foal Damascus, being neither difficult, quirky, nor exceptional, made little impression on his handlers at Jonabell Farm. "This situation of nobody having any clear memory of Damascus as a young horse is kind of similar to the middle child of a family turning out to be a superstar," said Benny Bell Williams, daughter of Jonabell founder John A. Bell III.

Damascus was weaned in the fall of 1964, and in keeping with the Bancroft horses' regimen, was shipped to Harold Polk's Polk-a-Dot Farm in Middleburg, Virginia. There he was broken as a yearling in 1965 and sent to Dorothy N. Lee's training center, also in Middleburg, in early 1966 to begin his preparations for the races. Mrs. Lee was well known as a horsewoman in the Maryland/Virginia region, and owners and trainers from the area routinely sent young horses to her.

A good-looking bay, Damascus grew to be taller than his sire, eventually standing sixteen hands. As a yearling, he was named after Damascus steel. Originating in Damascus, Syria, this type of steel is noted for its hardness, beautiful texture, and resiliency and is especially valued for making sword blades. The name particularly suited a son of Sword Dancer and a grandson of Blade of Time. Although stories circulated that Mrs. Bancroft named Damascus for a city in Maryland, her son, Thomas Jr., confirmed the name's origins.

Damascus and the other Bancroft horses based in Virginia received regular visits from their owners, who had a farm, Pen-Y-Bryn, close to Middleburg. In Welsh, Pen-Y-Bryn means "at the top of the hill," and the Bancrofts' farm was indeed on top of a ridge that overlooked a valley. The Bancrofts divided their time between their home on Long Island and the farm.

In the early 1960s the Bancrofts heeded friends' glowing recommendations and hired Frank Y. Whiteley Jr. as their trainer. Whiteley's base of operations in nearby Maryland reinforced the choice.

Whiteley had spent most his life involved in Thoroughbred racing and was already a nationally recognized trainer. He was born in Centreville on Maryland's Eastern Shore in 1915, the son of a prominent farmer who raised dairy cattle, horses, and mules, and grew corn and wheat. Whiteley's father also followed Thoroughbred racing.

The younger Whiteley developed a keen interest in horses as a child and started riding a Shetland pony on his father's farm. When Whiteley was ten, his father purchased a yearling colt for him. Whiteley patiently worked with the colt and broke him on his own. At first interested in becoming a jockey, Whiteley grew too tall and decided to train Thoroughbred horses instead, starting with "hundred dollar horses." He got his training license at eighteen and started working with horses at fairs, then advanced through the ranks from training claimers to developing standout Thoroughbreds.

Whiteley first gained recognition while training stakes winners Bronze Babu and Polarity for Mr. and Mrs. Ephraim Winer's Hill-N-Dale Farm, a Maryland-based stable. He later trained for Raymond Guest, the U.S. ambassador to Ireland and owner of Chieftain and Tom Rolfe. The gritty and gallant Tom Rolfe became the star of the

Guest stable, winning the 1965 Preakness and earning champion three-year-old colt honors. Under Whiteley's tutelage Chieftain won such stakes as the Cowdin and Tremont and the Arlington Handicap and Laurel Turf Cup.

Whiteley was considered an "old school" trainer. He pushed his horses, and his employees, hard but kept their best interest at heart. The money was important, but the horses always came first.

Whiteley's first successes for the Bancroft stable were with stakes-placed Aunt Tilt and stakes winner Hedevar, who defeated champions Tosmah and Bold Bidder in the 1966 Equipoise Mile while equaling the world record (1:33 1/5).

Whiteley recalled that Hedevar was the last horse Mrs. Bancroft saw run in the Belair colors before she developed Alzheimer's disease in her late fifties. Sadly, the illness, about which much less was known at that time, would keep her from being involved in the career of the most successful horse she ever bred and owned — Damascus.

Her husband, Thomas Bancroft Sr., and her mother, Elsie Woodward, continued Mrs. Bancroft's dream. They took more active roles with Damascus and the rest of the stable, and though Mrs. Bancroft was still the owner of record, Thomas Bancroft Sr. served as manager of the stable, spokesman for the family, and often led Damascus into the winner's circle. Elsie Woodward, co-owner and "silent partner," served as adviser, took part in winner's circle ceremonies, and sometimes spoke to the media about Damascus. Occasionally, the two Bancroft sons, Thomas Jr. and William, who were in their thirties at the time, would be on hand to see Damascus race.

Like his sire, Damascus was a late developer and didn't get to the races until September of 1966, his two-year-old year. Early in his training, Damascus impressed Whiteley, who admired Damascus' intelligence and the way the colt seemed to know what was expected of him. After he got to know Damascus, the trainer commented to the *Daily Racing Form*'s now defunct sister publication, the *Morning Telegraph*, that Damascus was healthy and easygoing with no bad habits and was "what you'd call a perfect horse around the barn." As far as his workouts, Whiteley told the author, "If you wanted him to work good, he'd do anything you wanted him to do. He'd work anyway you wanted him to go."

Damascus caught the tail end of the 1966 season. The star that year was undoubtedly Ogden Phipps' Buckpasser. Though an injury kept him out of the Triple Crown races, Buckpasser put together a winning streak that included the Travers, Woodward, and Jockey Club Gold Cup on his way to becoming a unanimous choice for Horse of the Year and champion three-year-old colt. Lady Pitt, Sword Dancer's 1963 filly out of Rock Drill, would become three-year-old filly champion; and Tom Rolfe was completing his last season before retirement. It was an especially good year for two-year-old colts, and Wheatley Stable's Successor and Tartan Farms' powerful and swift Dr. Fager led as contenders for the divisional championship.

From May through September, Damascus prepared for his first start. Whiteley noted, "His workouts were good. We knew he could run." When the time came to select a jockey, Whiteley had in mind Bill Shoemaker, who was riding Damascus' stablemate Tom Rolfe. Whiteley said to William G. Munn of the *Thoroughbred Record*, "I told (Shoemaker) that I had a two-year-old that could run a bit and I wanted him to ride it."

The Hall of Fame rider agreed to take the assignment. Shoemaker, who began his career in 1949, was the leading money-winning jockey for ten years: 1951, 1953, 1954, and then consecutively from 1958 to 1964. He had ridden racing headliners and champions such as Swaps, Round Table, Intentionally, Never Bend, Gallant Man, Jaipur, Cicada, Candy Spots, Northern Dancer, and Damascus' sire Sword Dancer. Additionally, the jockey had won the Kentucky Derby three times, the Preakness once, and the Belmont three times, including with Sword Dancer. Shoemaker learned more about the two-year-old Damascus prior to the youngster's first race by exercising him in the morning several times.

On September 28 at Aqueduct, Damascus went to the post for the first time, in a seven-furlong race for maiden two-year-old colts. For his first and subsequent starts, Damascus was equipped with a "D" bit and a narrow white band over his nose.

"I went to the jocks' room before the race and told him (Shoemaker) not to abuse him because I thought he was a pretty nice kind of colt," Whiteley told Munn.

During the race Damascus ran greenly, mostly gawking at his surroundings. He finished second, but as Whiteley said, "The race did him a lot of good." The winning colt was King Ranch's Comprador, a longshot who subsequently faded into obscurity.

Shoemaker recalled that Damascus had a "very laid back kind of disposition as a two-year-old." He said he thought Damascus should have won his first race but recollected that the colt had a tendency to linger at the gate.

Whiteley's and Shoemaker's confidence in the colt was rewarded two weeks later in another seven-furlong race at Aqueduct. Against a rather crowded field of juvenile colts, Damascus broke well, took an early lead, then drew away in the stretch to win by an impressive eight lengths in 1:24 3/5. He easily defeated Winslow Homer and Gun Mount, who would only be remembered for pursuing Damascus in his first victory. Joe Nichols of the *New York Times* noticed Damascus' maiden win and wrote, "Damascus...was the standout in the race, indeed, on the entire program."

Next, Whiteley found an allowance race for Damascus at Laurel Race Course on October 29. Fans at Laurel that crisp autumn day had the good fortune to see some of the best two-year-olds in America on the same race card. In addition to the up-and-coming

45

Damascus, champion two-year-old pro tem Successor and In Reality were competing in the featured stakes race of the day, the Pimlico Futurity. Shoemaker was in the enviable position of riding two outstanding juvenile colts that day: not only was he riding Damascus in the allowance race, but he also was aboard Successor for the Pimlico Futurity.

Successor was running at Laurel fresh from his triumph over Dr. Fager in the October 15 Champagne Stakes, and In Reality was a flashy colt who had lost by only three-quarters of a length, also to Dr. Fager, in the October 5 Cowdin Stakes. Successor had been third in the Cowdin.

In the Pimlico Futurity, In Reality upset favored Successor, but Damascus thrilled fans by winning his allowance race. He led every step of the way to win by twelve lengths, running the seven furlongs in 1:25 1/5.

Whiteley commented for the *Thoroughbred Record*, "After the race, Shoemaker told the reporters that I put him in the wrong race; he should have been in the Futurity instead." Damascus would conclude his two-year-old campaign in a stakes race, the Remsen.

In the meantime, the press was paying increasing attention to Damascus. The *Morning Telegraph*'s Teddy

Cox was one of his biggest boosters. A few days after Damascus' smashing Laurel race, Cox predicted, "One of the eye-catchers of the early phase of this meeting is Damascus who could become a top-flight 3-year-old next season under the able handling of Frank Y. Whiteley, Jr."

Though Damascus was eligible for the rich Garden State Stakes, Whiteley declined and opted instead for the one-mile Remsen on November 30 at Aqueduct. The Remsen, though run relatively late each year, still generally attracted talented two-year-old colts, and its past winners included champions and classic winners Northern Dancer and Carry Back. Because Shoemaker was so impressed with Damascus, he interrupted a vacation and flew in to ride the colt in his first stakes race.

The Remsen helped Whiteley assess the colt against better competition. Among the fourteen entrants were the promising Native Guile and Reflected Glory and the Canadian champion Cool Reception, who had won four stakes in his native country.

On a cool, clear day, a crowd of 23,347 installed Damascus as the 13-10 favorite. Native Guile broke first but was overtaken by a longshot, Yarak, as

Damascus gained position on the rail in behind the leaders. Yarak completed the half-mile in :46 but began running out of steam as Damascus moved into second. High Tribute, under Larry Adams, moved to the lead on the outside and appeared to have Damascus and Shoemaker boxed in on the rail as they turned for home. It looked like Shoemaker would have to take Damascus to another path, but High Tribute gave way and drifted out, allowing Shoemaker to gun his colt to the lead. Damascus pulled away to win by one and a half lengths with Native Guile finishing second and a late-running Reflected Glory closing for third. Damascus' winning time on a good track was 1:37.

Shoemaker was very enthusiastic about Damascus and the Remsen victory. After dismounting in the winner's circle, the jockey asked Whiteley, "What are you going to do with him now?"

The trainer said, "I'm not going to do anything with him until next spring."

To that Shoemaker replied, "Well, just keep in touch with me."

After the Remsen, racing fans, horsemen, and the media considered Damascus to be a horse to watch in next season's spring classics. Handicapper Tommy Trotter thought enough of the lightly raced Sword Dancer colt to assign him 119 pounds on the Experimental Free Handicap for two-year-olds. The highweights on the 1966 Free Handicap were champion two-year-old colt Successor, with 126 pounds, and Dr. Fager, with 125. After the Remsen, Whiteley sent Damascus back to Mrs. Lee's farm for a rest before the colt's three-year-old campaign.

DAMASCUS

CHAPTER 4

A Rivalry Begins

D amascus enjoyed a short break at Mrs. Lee's Middleburg farm before he shipped to Whiteley's training barn in Camden, South Carolina. The colt resumed light training in the weeks before the Whiteley stable moved north.

The trainer planned to run Damascus in the New York series of stakes for three-year-olds, with the Bay Shore Stakes on March 25 being the first target after a prep race.

Whiteley thought a six-furlong allowance race at Pimlico on March 11 looked like an ideal prep, and he contacted veteran Maryland jockey Nick Shuk to ride Damascus, not wanting to bring Shoemaker in from California for a non-stakes event. The track was listed as fast, but showers had left some puddles. Damascus broke from the outside, and not very sharply, and was kept wide for much of the race. Seeing three puddles in front of him, Damascus instinctively jumped them. As he leapt over the last one, Damascus was hit and knocked sideways by Coral King. He quickly recovered and overtook the leader, Solar Bomb, who bumped him at the finish as Damascus beat him by a head. The time of the six-furlong race was 1:12 1/5. Damascus won admirers that day for courageously overcoming adversity in what had been the toughest race of his career thus far.

The New York series of stakes for Triple Crown hopefuls began March 13, with the running of the Swift Stakes, and all eyes were on 1966's champion two-year-old and early Kentucky Derby winter book favorite, Successor. The winner, however, was a roan son of First Landing named Solo Landing, who had already won the Laurel New Year's Handicap and Francis Scott Key Stakes. Successor finished a disappointing fourth, compromising his status as the leading contender for the Triple Crown races. He was sent to Kentucky to prepare for the Blue Grass Stakes in April.

Another formidable colt needing a spot to run was Dr. Fager, the runner-up to Successor as best two-year-old colt. Owned by Tartan Stable and trained by John Nerud, Dr. Fager had won four of five starts at two, his only loss being to Successor in the Champagne Stakes. Dr. Fager was nominated for the seven-furlong Bay Shore Stakes but would not make his first start until the Gotham.

In the March 25 Bay Shore, Damascus faced the promising Solo Landing, Disciplinarian, and Nehoc's Bullet on a muddy track. Because of his winning streak and vanquishing of Successor in the Swift, Solo Landing was the morning-line favorite. Bill Shoemaker returned as Damascus' rider, demonstrating how highly he regarded the colt by choosing to ride him over the outstanding older horse Pretense in the Gulfstream Park Handicap in Florida. John Sellers would ride Pretense to victory that day.

Damascus disliked the mud clods hitting him in the face as he tracked leaders Disciplinarian and Solo Landing. But Shoemaker had the colt settled into a smooth stride when Damascus made his move from fourth place in the stretch and swept by Disciplinarian and Nehoc's Bullet to win by two and a half lengths. He ran the seven furlongs in 1:25 4/5. The race impressed

Charles Hatton of the *Morning Telegraph*, who wrote that Damascus had "the will to win that makes a champion."

The next race on the calendar for the leading New York-based three-year-old colts was the one-mile Gotham on April 15. Because of snowstorms and a horsemen's strike at Aqueduct, Nerud had had difficulty finding a suitable allowance race for Dr. Fager. Instead, Dr. Fager prepped for the Gotham in a public workout between races on April 3 during which he raced against his half brother Aforethought and Gaylord's Feather. Aqueduct race goers watched as Dr. Fager finished a length in front of his stablemates in a swift 1:10 1/5 for six furlongs. Shoemaker had ridden Dr. Fager in the Cowdin and Champagne, but since Shoemaker had become the regular rider of Damascus, Nerud selected jockey Manuel Ycaza to ride Dr. Fager in the Gotham Stakes.

Dr. Fager and Damascus were installed as co-favorites for the Gotham, with odds of 13-10. A crowd of 50,522 turned out at Aqueduct in hopes of seeing these two outstanding colts battle it out. They were not disappointed. At the start Damascus uncharacteristically shot to the lead from his outside post position but was overtaken by Royal Malabar, who opened up by three lengths as the horses reached the far turn. Damascus started to chase after the leader, and Dr. Fager began moving on the outside. Overtaking Royal Malabar, Damascus gained the lead, but Dr. Fager was soon on his right side, vying for the lead. Running head and head down the stretch, the two lived up to their equal odds by matching strides as they approached the finish line. Nearing the wire, Shoemaker pushed and whipped Damascus, but with the two colts in such close quarters, the jockey could only whip with his left hand. Dr. Fager then edged ahead first by a head, then a neck, and then a half-length to win the race. The time was 1:35 1/5. Fans who saw the race at the track and on television had just witnessed the first battle between these two titans, a rivalry that would be debated and discussed for years to come.

Shoemaker blamed himself for the loss and maintained he had given the Sword Dancer colt a disappointing ride, having Damascus too close to the pace early and later losing the advantage that the colt had had breaking from the outside. After the Gotham, Shoemaker said to Whiteley, "I got him beat, but Dr.

Fager will never beat Damascus again as long as I'm on him." As it turned out, Shoemaker would live up to his promise on that April day. Whiteley said years later, "Shoemaker was learning the horse and the horse was learning him." He added, "Dr. Fager was a good horse, too. He beat Damascus that day."

Thomas Bancroft Sr. commented to Charles Hatton after the race: "I was on the backstretch and saw the track there that day. Damascus had to run through a couple of acres of rough going to get on the racing strip. As for Shoemaker's part, you know these boys must make split-second decisions."

Those anticipating a rematch in the Wood Memorial the following week were disappointed. Nerud had already made his intentions about Dr. Fager known before the Gotham and reported to the *Morning Telegraph* that his colt would not start in the Wood. Instead, Nerud decided to send Dr. Fager's stablemate Brunch, Tartan Farms' undefeated son of Intentionally and Munch. As for Dr. Fager, Nerud indicated the colt might be better suited to the mile and three-sixteenths Preakness than the mile and a quarter Kentucky Derby.

On April 22 nine three-year-olds contested the mile and one-eighth Wood Memorial, the final New York prep for the Kentucky Derby, before a crowd of 50,521. Facing Damascus, the 7-10 favorite, were Brunch; the speedy Royal Malabar; Dawn Glory, a star in Puerto Rico; Gala Performance, a well-regarded horse from the Alfred G. Vanderbilt barn; and outsiders Proviso, Puntador, High Hat, and Blasting Charge. Shoemaker was quoted in the *New York Times* about his strategy for the race: "I'll try to take hold of him early. Then I'll put him to work in the stretch, because if he's going to win the Derby, that's the way he's going to have to do it."

In the Wood, Brunch and Gala Performance took the lead and ran as a team around the first turn. Dawn Glory followed, and Damascus was rated in fourth. Gala Performance then took over the lead from a fading Brunch, with Dawn Glory still in pursuit and Damascus still content, sitting in fourth. Around the final turn Shoemaker turned Damascus loose, and the favorite flew by the leaders to win going away by six lengths in 1:49 3/5. Gala Performance was second, and Dawn Glory finished third. "I haven't changed my opinion. His race was as good as the Gotham, but I

guess that the big difference was that I rode him differ-
ently," said Shoemaker after the race. "This time I
eased Damascus back early. In the Gotham he broke
good and I let him go. Then, he got rank."

Shoemaker was full of optimism about Damascus'
chances in the Kentucky Derby. Whiteley, though,
kept his Derby card close to the chest, declining to con-
firm that Damascus would run next in Kentucky.

CHAPTER 5

A Colt For The Classics

E ighteen years had passed since Citation won the Triple Crown in 1948. Some horses had come close. For instance, Native Dancer and Nashua each lost the Kentucky Derby but won the Preakness and the Belmont while Tim Tam, Carry Back, and Northern Dancer all won the Derby and Preakness only to be defeated in the Belmont. After his sterling performance in the Wood Memorial, Damascus was favored to win the 1967 Kentucky Derby and hopefully sweep the next two jewels of the Triple Crown.

It was a year of talented colts, and racing writers would report later that it was perhaps the best crop since the previous decade's powerhouse trio of Bold Ruler, Gallant Man, and Round Table. In addition to Damascus and Dr. Fager, there was In Reality, a bay son of two champions, Intentionally and My Dear Girl, owned and bred by Frances Genter, trained by Melvin "Sunshine" Calvert, and named for one of his trainer's favorite phrases. In Reality took the Florida route to the classics and won the Hibiscus Stakes, placed in the Florida Breeders' Handicap and Flamingo Stakes, then came back to win the Florida Derby. Like Dr. Fager, In Reality would not be entered in the Kentucky Derby but was a possibility for the Preakness Stakes.

The colts that would oppose Damascus in the Kentucky Derby ranged from lightly raced hopefuls to heavily campaigned horses. Successor, the previous year's champion, had not won as a three-year-old and most recently had finished fourth in the Blue Grass Stakes at Keeneland. Still, the connections of the bay son of leading sire Bold Ruler and champion Misty Morn hoped for a rebound in Louisville. Ruken, a highly regarded colt by Nashville, campaigned that year primarily in California, winning the Santa Anita Derby. He came east for the Keeneland meet and defeated Successor in an allowance race. Diplomat Way, a son of Nashua, won the Blue Grass Stakes and finished second in the Louisiana Derby; heavily campaigned, the colt already had twenty-one races under his girth. Other major contenders included Derby Trial winner Barbs Delight, California Derby victor Reason to Hail, and Louisiana Derby winner Ask the Fare. Other contenders in the race included Proud Clarion, who had finished second to Diplomat Way in the Blue Grass; Puerto Rican star Dawn Glory; and longshots Field Master, Gentleman James, Lightning Orphan, Second Encounter, and Dr. Isby. All of these colts would be required for the first time in their young lives to run one and a quarter miles.

The excitement of the upcoming Derby was tempered with some anxiety. During the weeks before the race, civil rights demonstrations, boycotts, and marches had taken place in Louisville. The demonstrators were pushing for a city ordinance allowing African Americans to live in non-segregated communities and to have equal housing rights. Several of the demonstrations had sparked racial violence in the city throughout the spring. At Churchill Downs a few protestors ran in front of horses during the first race on May 2; this led to the National Guardsmen being called out to the racetrack — where they would remain for the running of the Kentucky Derby on May 6. As

Frank Whiteley described the atmosphere in Louisville before the 1967 Derby: "Everything was in an uproar down there."

Damascus arrived at Churchill Downs on April 24, and as the favorite he was hounded by the press, creating more stress for the colt and his connections. Whiteley told reporters he was pleased with Damascus' first workout at the track, on April 29. The colt breezed six furlongs in 1:19, and Whiteley reported Damascus was coming up to the race "very nicely." Subsequently, the Sword Dancer colt worked on May 2, clocking one and one-eighth miles on a sloppy track in 1:54.

Damascus drew post position two, displeasing Whiteley, who later commented, "These inside post positions are murder." As post time drew near, Whiteley led Damascus from his barn to the paddock area. The trainer noticed the colt suddenly becoming high strung.

"I don't know what got him stirred up, but he got stirred up. He was nervous before he got to the paddock. In the barn he was okay," Whiteley recalled, adding, "I was tense. You can pass that onto your horse."

The noise of the crowd contributed to Damascus' agitation as he headed for the paddock. Once inside, Whiteley noted his colt becoming even edgier. The usually calm, cool, and collected Damascus uncharacteristically pinned back his ears and kicked, broke out in a sweat, and looked nervous as he was saddled for the race. Thomas Bancroft Sr. later observed: "He was in a state in the paddock stall. Kicking and sweating between the legs. I never saw him behave that way before." As the band played a very loud rendition of "My Old Kentucky Home," Damascus' agitated state intensified. He sweated, rolled his eyes, and fought his jockey during the post parade, spurring an outrider to take the fractious colt in hand.

Whiteley, who had taken a seat in the stands, peered through binoculars to watch the break. He could tell that Damascus was still having problems. Though the colt broke well, Whiteley observed that Damascus did not settle down to his usually smooth stride and was visibly fighting his jockey, not allowing Shoemaker to rate him. Even that early in the race Whiteley knew they were beaten. "You can't fight a horse going a mile and one-quarter," he said.

Barbs Delight was the early leader, followed by Dawn Glory, Diplomat Way, and Damascus, who raced along the rail in fourth. Dawn Glory moved alongside Barbs Delight around the first turn, followed by Diplomat Way and Damascus. In the backstretch Dawn Glory started to fade, and Diplomat Way moved into second, with Damascus about three lengths off the group. Toward the back of the pack was Proud Clarion, saving ground in eighth place, ahead of Ruken and Successor, who both appeared to have no chance.

Turning for home, Barbs Delight showed no sign of quitting, but Diplomat Way and Dawn Glory started to fade. Shoemaker set down Damascus for his drive. With Barbs Delight still in command, Damascus took off after him, while Proud Clarion, ridden by Bob Ussery, began closing from the back. In the stretch Proud Clarion moved forcefully enough to pass Damascus. With every stride Proud Clarion narrowed the gap to the leader, Barbs Delight. Barbs Delight dug in, giving his all, but Proud Clarion got by him to win by a length, with Barbs Delight three lengths ahead of Damascus, who hung in the stretch. Proud Clarion, who had gone off at 30-1, paid $62.20 to win and surprised the fans who had made Damascus the overwhelming favorite and Ruken and Successor the second choices. Successor had closed for sixth, and Ruken ended up eighth.

After the race Whiteley told the press, "I guess you could say I am disappointed, but not discouraged. In any event, we are going to run back in the Preakness."

Damascus' other connections were equally upset with the outcome. Groom Walter Furr stated, "I guess I was just plain mad because he got beat in the Kentucky Derby. It broke my heart to see the best horse get beat and I certainly couldn't take it." Despite the loss, Furr praised the Sword Dancer colt: "I've never been around one who eats so well and does so well. It's unbelievable. I don't think he's missed a single oat since he was broken as a yearling. He has never had a blemish on him of any kind, not even bucked shins. If there ever was the perfect horse, Damascus is it."

When Whiteley asked Shoemaker if the jockey would ride Damascus in the Preakness, Shoemaker replied, "If you can get him to the paddock quiet, I'll not only ride him, I'll win it." Damascus departed

Louisville on May 8 via a horse van headed to Laurel Race Course in Maryland. "I couldn't obtain a favorable plane schedule, so I just hopped aboard the van," Whiteley told the *Morning Telegraph*. "It was a pretty rough trip; these vans are not made for Pullman comfort." After his arrival at Laurel, Damascus became his old self. He lay down in his stall and took a nap. "He's a mighty intelligent colt," observed Whiteley. "He knows the art of relaxation. That's why I knew he was in trouble when he became stirred up at Derby time."

Whiteley set about getting Damascus ready for the May 20 Preakness. The colt would now have someone to escort him to the paddock and the post parade for his next races. Duffy, a Whiteley stable pony who accompanied racehorses to the track in the mornings, was deputized for the job. He immediately had a pronounced calming influence on the racehorse. Several racing reporters later speculated that a major reason for Damascus' attack of nerves at the Derby was that he missed his pal Duffy. From the Preakness on, Duffy became a familiar sight, accompanying Damascus to the post and keeping him mellow. Legendary sports columnist Red Smith called Duffy "friend and comforter and father confessor" to Damascus.

Whiteley had sent Damascus to Churchill Downs within days of the colt's triumph in the Wood Memorial. For the Preakness, Whiteley decided to change tactics and sent Damascus to Pimlico, some thirty minutes away from Laurel, on the morning of the race. Whiteley wanted to keep him away from the throngs of reporters and circus-like atmosphere that had set the colt on edge in Louisville.

As Damascus prepared to avenge his Derby loss, Nerud announced to disappointed fans that Dr. Fager would not compete in the Preakness. Melvin Calvert, meanwhile, had decided to send In Reality to Pimlico. Proud Clarion, whose previous victory would make him less of a longshot, was also entered, along with Derby runner-up Barbs Delight; the speedy Bold Ruler colt, Great Power; Misty Cloud; Favorable Turn; Ask the Fare; and another Whiteley-trained colt, Orme Wilson Jr.'s Celtic Air, who would run as an entry with Damascus. The Sword Dancer colt was favored despite his Derby performance, with Barbs Delight the second choice and Proud Clarion and In Reality getting support as co-third choices. The Preakness, at one and three-sixteenths miles, was shorter than the Derby, but the colts would be going around Pimlico's rather sharp turns, which had given some horses trouble in previous runnings.

About a half hour before the race, all the horses except Damascus and Celtic Air had appeared in the infield saddling area used for the Preakness. The delay was such that most horses were already saddled, and an outrider had to go to the barn to locate Whiteley and Damascus. Kent Hollingsworth for *The Blood-Horse* wrote: "There was some talk about Whiteley's tardiness, but his son David saddled Celtic Air, and Whiteley quickly saddled Damascus; steward J. Fred Colwill checked the clock and Whiteley had brought his horses to the paddock 20 minutes before post time, within the rule." This tactic seemed to work with Damascus, and he showed none of the paddock obstreperousness he had displayed in Louisville. Whiteley was pleased with Damascus' demeanor. "He didn't have a wet hair on him when he left the paddock. He was relaxed, and you have to have a relaxed horse to win a race like this," said the trainer.

Damascus, comforted by Duffy's presence, went

calmly to the post, seemingly unbothered by the band playing the state song "Maryland, My Maryland." Soon after the gate clanged open, Celtic Air took the lead, and Great Power quickly challenged him. Barbs Delight stayed close to the leaders. Around the first turn In Reality was saving ground on the inside in seventh, with Damascus in ninth, and Proud Clarion trailing. Down the backstretch, Celtic Air pulled ahead by two lengths, followed by Barbs Delight, who passed a tiring Great Power.

Damascus, In Reality, and Proud Clarion were still being restrained by their jockeys and were in position to start their moves. As he headed into the final turn and began edging Damascus closer to the leaders, Shoemaker noticed Proud Clarion pulling closer. "I sort of thought Proud Clarion was the horse to beat, and I wasn't about to let him get in front of me if I could help it," said Shoemaker afterwards. Coming to the three-eighths pole, Celtic Air was calling it a day. Barbs Delight took over the lead, followed by Misty Cloud and Favorable Turn. Eight horses were clustered within four lengths of each other, some in tight quarters. Shoemaker took Damascus to the outside around the turn, with Proud Clarion also making his bid right behind him. Shoemaker urged on Damascus, hitting him six times with the whip down the stretch. The colt responded, winning the race by two and a quarter lengths. The final time was a fast 1:55 1/5, the second-fastest Preakness since the race began being run at a mile and three-sixteenths in 1925 (Nashua had the fastest time with 1:54 3/5). In Reality came on in the stretch to beat Proud Clarion for second place by four lengths.

After the race a jubilant Shoemaker told reporters, "He had a bigger punch today. He liked the track and everything. And he was more relaxed." The jockey added: "This is definitely a Belmont Stakes horse. He ran the race I knew he could run. I looked back and when I saw Proud Clarion coming on in back of me, I really got busy and belted my horse pretty good. The colt wasn't as shook up as he was for the Derby when I couldn't get him under control during the early part. This time I moved when I figured the time was best. I must confess, though, that I lost a lot of ground, but as we came toward the stretch there was no place to go except the outside. I also had a helluva horse under me."

The third jewel of the Triple Crown, the Belmont Stakes, would be run at Aqueduct Racetrack on June 3. Construction of a new grandstand had closed Belmont Park, which would reopen in 1968. The race was instead run during what was called the "Belmont at Aqueduct" meeting. The Belmont was a demanding race for three-year-olds, requiring them to run one and a half miles, the longest distance run thus far in their careers.

Whiteley continued his expert handling of Damascus as he prepared him for the Belmont from his Delaware Park base. Whiteley's training regimen for the colt included walking him around a shady area and spraying his legs with water from a garden hose. This treatment generally lasted between forty-five minutes and an hour. Afterward, Damascus was given time to graze. Whiteley explained he did this because "horses get nervous and tired of being penned in those stalls. It really isn't natural for them. So, if you can spare the time to hose them and graze them, you might be lucky enough to have a more relaxed horse." Whiteley's regimen worked for Damascus, who remained very poised and calm for the Belmont Stakes.

At Delaware Park the day before the Belmont, Damascus was given a final workout of three furlongs in :37 3/5 and then was shipped to Aqueduct. All seemed well the morning of the race, and as Kent Hollingsworth reported, "...Damascus appeared well-settled, enjoying the rock 'n roll music coming from a radio at his stall door."

The colts facing Damascus, again the favorite, that day were a talented lot: Canadian star Cool Reception, Proud Clarion, speedy Prinkipo, Gentleman James, and the durable Reason to Hail. Longshots Blasting Charge, Gaylord's Feather, Favorable Turn, and Nehoc's Bullet, another son of Sword Dancer, also lined up to face the Preakness winner, although Nehoc's Bullet later scratched.

At the start Prinkipo and Cool Reception quickly took the lead as expected, with Favorable Turn and Reason to Hail in pursuit. As they passed the stands at Aqueduct for the first time, Damascus appeared rank but was taken in hand by Shoemaker and settled in fifth going around the turn to the backstretch. Down the backstretch Cool Reception took the lead, followed by Prinkipo, Favorable Turn, Proud Clarion, and

Damascus. Jockey Braulio Baeza, who replaced Bob Ussery on Proud Clarion, moved on the leaders as they headed for the final turn. Shoemaker sent Damascus on the outside, driving after Proud Clarion and the others. Proud Clarion briefly passed Cool Reception heading into the stretch but tired, and the Canadian colt again took the lead. Shoemaker urged on Damascus at the quarter pole, whipping him right-handed. His mount passed the tiring Proud Clarion and took aim at Cool Reception. Damascus pulled even with that colt, then put him away to win by two and a half lengths. Gentleman James made a big run to finish third, a half-length behind Cool Reception. The time of the race was 2:28 4/5.

Tragically, Cool Reception fractured his right fore cannon bone near the end of the Belmont. His jockey, John Sellers, told the press, "My horse ran the last six-teenth on guts alone." Track veterinarian William O. Reed operated on the colt and placed three pins in the fractured bone. It looked like the colt would be saved for stud and have the chance to pass on his courage to his offspring. However, events took a turn for the worse. When Cool Reception got to his feet after the operation, he completely shattered the bone and had to be euthanized.

With the Belmont Stakes, Damascus had won two of the three jewels of the Triple Crown. In so doing, he joined Native Dancer and Nashua in winning the final two legs but having had the misfortune of losing the Derby. But like his champion counterparts, Damascus still had many other races, challenges — and glories — awaiting him.

CHAPTER 6

A Summer Of Success

The summer of 1967 would prove triumphant for Damascus, and it would be a memorable season for racing fans. In addition to Damascus' feats on the track, fans would be treated to the racing exploits of the mighty Buckpasser, who thrilled race goers with his stretch runs under high imposts; the lightning-fast colt Dr. Fager; the consistent In Reality; the gallant mare Straight Deal; the talented three-year-old filly Furl Sail; and the accomplished four-year-old colt Handsome Boy.

A question many Turf devotees, writers, and horse-men asked that summer was: When would Damascus and Dr. Fager meet again to settle the best three-year-old colt title? Indeed, the question would burn throughout the summer months. In his Preakness and Belmont victories, Damascus had won convincingly over the best three-year-old colts in the nation, save one, Dr. Fager. To win the title, he would need to avenge his Gotham Stakes loss to Dr. Fager. Since the Gotham, Dr. Fager had easily won the Withers Stakes and had finished first in the Jersey Derby, only to be disqualified by stewards for interference in the stretch and placed fourth to In Reality.

This highly anticipated rematch could have occurred as early as June 24 in the mile Arlington Classic at Arlington Park; Nerud and Whiteley were both considering this race for their respective colts. However, the proverbial "fly in the ointment" came when Whiteley discovered that Damascus would be required to spot Dr. Fager six pounds under the allowance conditions of the Classic.

"We're passing the Chicago race," Whiteley told the *Morning Telegraph.* "We're not avoiding Dr. Fager, but I feel that if we are to meet him, and this is inevitable, we'll meet him on an even basis." Dr. Fager, ridden by Braulio Baeza, went on to win the Classic by ten lengths.

For Damascus' next start, Whiteley opted instead for the June 17 Leonard Richards Stakes at Delaware Park. Whiteley told the press that Delaware Park "does so much for the comfort and well-being of the horse" and added that "Delaware Park...deserved to have Damascus in a stake. We make our headquarters there during the summer and we're treated royally."

Damascus went into the Leonard Richards without Shoemaker, who was serving a five-day suspension, which would begin on the same day as the race. Shoemaker was set down by Hollywood Park stewards for letting his mount cut across in the stretch and inter- fere with the other horses in the race. Consequently, Whiteley contacted Ron Turcotte, who had ridden Tom Rolfe to victory in the 1965 Preakness for Whiteley. Turcotte told *The Blood-Horse*: "I've never ridden Damascus but when I learned I was riding him, I stud- ied films of the Belmont and Wood Memorial...When I was asked to ride him, it didn't take me long to say 'yes.' He looks like an easy horse to ride. You can rate him easy, or take him to the front; he just does every- thing you ask him to do."

Damascus' opposition in the Leonard Richards included Misty Cloud, who had won the E. Palmer Heagerty Stakes and Annapolis Stakes, and Favorable Turn, who had won the Saratoga Special as a two-year-old. Favorable Turn took the lead at the break, followed by Misty Cloud with Damascus rated in fourth. Turcotte later said, "He felt really good coming out of the gate. I had a hold on him, because I didn't want to break on the lead. When Damascus brought his head up, like he understood what I meant, I released my hold and relaxed." At the half-mile, Turcotte urged Damascus into third, and at the head of the stretch, he shot past Favorable Turn. "I tapped him with the whip on the right side at the eighth pole because Mr. Whiteley told me Damascus has a tendency to loaf on the lead," Turcotte said afterward. "It was an easy race all the way. I was holding him back going across the finish line because he was winning easily. It probably was the easiest race he ever ran. I never was on a horse that did so many things right. Anywhere you want to move he'll go, then slow down and rate himself...It was a terrific feeling to ride a great one. I hope I can do it again." Damascus' margin of victory was three and a quarter lengths over Misty Cloud, and he ran the one and one-eighth miles in 1:49 1/5.

Even though Turcotte rode Damascus in only one other race, the colt left an indelible impression. Turcotte told the author in 2002: "I had ridden great horses like Northern Dancer and Tom Rolfe. But when I got on Damascus he was by far the best that I had sat on at the time. I mean as far as maneuverability, the way he would make sudden moves when you called on him...just like you'd step on a gas pedal of a car and it accelerates real fast. That's how he accelerated...Today, I'd have to place him second to the top horse I rode, Secretariat."

A milestone for any three-year-old colt is taking on his elders for the first time. The William du Pont Jr. Handicap on July 8 marked such a milestone for Damascus. And he was giving the older horses weight. Damascus was assigned top weight of 121 pounds, conceding seven to eleven pounds. The competition included the five-year-old Rough'n Tumble horse Flag Raiser, a multiple stakes winner who had placed in the Royal Poinciana Handicap earlier that year and would go on to win the Atlantic City Handicap, and Exceedingly, who had won the City of Baltimore Handicap. Flag Raiser carried 114 pounds; Exceedingly, 113.

Shoemaker rejoined the Damascus camp, flying in from California for the race. Damascus was in a playful mood before the race and tried to dump his rider as the horses headed for the track. Flag Raiser set the pace, chased by Classic Work, Exceedingly, and Spiceberry. Damascus trailed. Around the turn Damascus started his move, but Exceedingly, farther up, began to run down Flag Raiser. At the head of the stretch, Exceedingly took the lead, followed by a surging Damascus. Observers watched in surprise as Exceedingly hung in and did not let the heavily favored Damascus pass him. The two were head and head for the lead and hit the wire together in a dramatic photo finish. Stewards proclaimed Exceedingly the winner by a nose in time of 1:42 1/5, and the longshot paid twenty-seven dollars to win.

Frank Whiteley later described the upset in the du Pont as "the same thing that happened in the Gotham. Shoemaker was trying to give him an easy race. He ran to that horse (Exceedingly) and eased up and Damascus stayed with that horse. You couldn't drive him (Damascus) away from him." Whiteley explained that once Damascus got next to another horse, he had to move past right away and not be given a breather. Reporters noted that Damascus' giving eight pounds to the older Exceedingly didn't exactly help matters.

Whiteley wasted no time getting Damascus back to the races, entering him a week later in the Dwyer Handicap at one and a quarter miles at Aqueduct. Damascus, a durable and healthy performer, was capable of returning in a week; this was not unheard of back in 1967 when major campaigners, including Handsome Boy, would, at times, race every week. Racing secretary Tommy Trotter assigned Damascus the colt's highest impost as a three-year-old: 128 pounds. Race day did not have an auspicious beginning. Whiteley was ill with a virus, and Shoemaker arrived late from California. It was a muggy morning, and Damascus was feeling the heat and acting restless.

The competition that day included the highly regarded Bold Hour, who had won the July 1 Saranac Handicap and would carry 125 pounds. Damascus' other foes in the Dwyer were Beau Apple, Favorable Turn, Air Rights, Fort Drum, Blasting Charge, High Tribute, and Biller. At the start of the race, Beau Apple, in light under 106 pounds, set the pace, with Favorable Turn and Air Rights close behind, followed by Bold Hour. Damascus was last going around the clubhouse turn and down the backstretch. Watching from the stands, Thomas Bancroft Sr. was uneasy. "I don't like to see the horse so far off the pace," he commented.

At the half-mile pole Shoemaker began his move on Damascus and gained on the leaders. Favorable Turn had the lead, and Ron Turcotte used his mount's sixteen-pound weight advantage to keep them ahead of the relentless Damascus. Shoemaker thought Damascus would roll right by Favorable Turn but realized that Turcotte had given the colt a stamina-saving ride. Damascus had to reach deep to pull ahead of his stubborn rival and managed to reach the wire first by three-quarters of a length in a relatively slow time of 2:03 over the sloppy track. Turcotte told reporters, "My horse ran a helluva race. He hung on like a bull. At the sixteenth pole I thought he was going to win, but that Damascus was too much."

As it turned out, Damascus and his rival Dr. Fager would both be in the headlines the next day since the latter colt posted a dazzling victory in the Rockingham Special Stakes on the same afternoon as the Dwyer. Dr. Fager set a track record of 1:48 1/5 in the one and one-eighth-mile race that day. Anticipation for a Damascus-

Dr. Fager rematch was in the air as John Nerud announced his colt would next start in the August 19 Travers Stakes, a race in which Whiteley was also considering running Damascus.

Three weeks later Damascus was back in action in the mile and one-eighth American Derby at Arlington Park. Once again he met In Reality and gave him weight. Damascus, carrying top weight of 126 pounds, also faced some challengers from the past, including Tumble Wind, Favorable Turn, Diplomat Way, Barbs Delight, and Gentleman James. Whiteley remembered that prior to the race he told Shoemaker he expected a big effort from the colt: "I'd like to see Damascus three-year-old of the year, if not Horse of the Year."

When the gates opened, Barbs Delight grabbed the lead, followed by Favorable Turn, Diplomat Way, Tumble Wind, In Reality, Damascus, and Gentleman James. Whiteley recalled that as he viewed the race and saw Damascus heading down the backstretch way in the back of the pack. "I thought I made a terrible mistake (entering him)." Damascus gradually gained ground going toward the final turn, and as Whiteley put it, Damascus and Shoemaker "whipped around those horses." At the head of the stretch, Barbs Delight grittily held onto the lead, followed by Favorable Turn, Diplomat Way, and In Reality. Damascus cruised by the latter three and took aim on the leader. At the three-sixteenths pole, Damascus caught and passed Barbs Delight, and at that point the race was over. Damascus drew away to win by seven lengths and set a track record of 1:46 4/5. (The record stood until Spectacular Bid broke it in 1980.) In Reality closed for second, ahead of Damascus' Dwyer rival, Favorable Turn. After the race, Shoemaker told the press: "I had to use my whip on him quite a bit (seven times), but this is not unusual with Damascus. He loafs so much until you get his mind on running. He was really at his peak in this one." Whiteley observed that that was the way Damascus liked to run. "That's the way Shoemaker rode him. That's why he knew how to ride him," he said.

Damascus' dazzling running style, which just kept improving as he matured and as he classically demonstrated in the American Derby, was perhaps best described by William H. Rudy in *Racing in America, 1960–1979*: "Damascus was a plain-looking colt of average size...his character marked by a lack of flash and fire

— up to a certain point. That point usually came on the turn for home or in the upper stretch where with exciting low action and with catlike grace, he blew by his opposition. No horse of his time had a quicker move."

For a time it looked as if Damascus and Dr. Fager were on a collision course to the Travers, but once again the much-anticipated match up was not to be; Nerud would instead run Dr. Fager in the New Hampshire Sweepstakes in early September. Three other colts showed up at Saratoga to face Damascus on Travers day: old opponents Reason to Hail and Gala Performance, and new foe Tumiga. Tumiga, a horse with early speed, had annexed the Carter and Gravesend handicaps and had finished second to Dr. Fager in the Withers Stakes. In addition to finishing second to Damascus in the Wood Memorial, Gala Performance, by Native Dancer, had won the Prince George's Stakes, Challedon Stakes, Jim Dandy Stakes, and Kent Stakes. The Travers, a prestigious race run at the classic distance of one and a quarter miles and known as the "Midsummer Derby," included such immortals of the Turf among its past winners as Man o' War, Whirlaway, Native Dancer, Gallant Man, and

Sword Dancer. Two of the most memorable Travers were arguably Jim Dandy's major upset of Triple Crown winner Gallant Fox in 1930 and Jaipur's nose triumph after battling the entire distance with Ridan in 1962.

Before the race Whiteley kept Damascus contented with rock music in his stall, drowning out the loud race calls and cheers of race fans at Saratoga, and with the routine grazing time outside in his paddock away from the confines of his stall. Red Smith reported for the *Washington Post* that, in addition to the companionship of Duffy, Damascus had recently made a friend of a rooster named Pete. One of Damascus' grooms, Bob Alston, told Smith, "Pete came from three barns away, flew in and perched over Damascus' stall. Man came and got (Pete), kept him penned up three days, and as soon as he turned him loose, the rooster came back to Damascus. Now if we ship the horse away without him, the bird has a fit."

Damascus benefited from the extra steps taken to ensure his comfort, and the colt entered the Travers in the best of shape.

The track was sloppy for Travers day, but the track condition didn't diminish the crowd's faith in

Damascus. As the four colts went to the post, Damascus was bet down to 1-5. When the gates opened, Tumiga and Gala Performance shot to the front and raced together to extend their lead over Damascus by fifteen lengths. Reason to Hail trailed. Those watching the race undoubtedly had the same thought: would Damascus be able to catch them? At the three-eighths pole, Damascus gave a clear answer, making his powerful run as Tumiga and Gala Performance began to tire visibly. Damascus easily swept by them and kept widening his lead, thrilling the crowd. At the finish he was twenty-two lengths ahead of Reason to Hail, with Tumiga third.

In winning the most impressive race of his career, Damascus equaled the Saratoga track record of 2:01 3/5, despite the sloppy track. "The crowd, even those who bet against (Damascus), greeted him with a mighty cheer at the wire and again when he came to the winner's circle," observed Joe Nichols of the *New York Times*. The crowd was in awe of the colt that had seemed totally out of the race but had caught up with the leaders and easily passed them to win.

An understandably ecstatic Shoemaker spoke to

reporters about the race and the talented colt: "I didn't know we equaled the track mark, or I might have let him run a bit more in the final furlong. I have to say he's as good as any horse I've ever ridden." When questioned about how far back Damascus was in the early stages, Shoemaker responded, "No, I wasn't worried when they were so far ahead. I had a lot of horse running real easy. When I asked him to move to the leaders just before we hit the half-mile pole, he took off. We had them by the three-eighths."

After a sensational summer campaign Damascus was a serious contender for champion three-year-old and Horse of the Year honors. However, since Damascus and Dr. Fager's paths never crossed that summer, a summit meeting was still in order, and fans and sports writers alike clamored for one. Damascus would have to meet and defeat Dr. Fager to become champion three-year-old colt. To be named Horse of the Year, he would have to defeat both Dr. Fager and defending champion Buckpasser. Inevitably, the day of reckoning would arrive.

CHAPTER 7

The Race Of The Century

By the time September 1967 arrived, the "Big Three" of Buckpasser, Damascus, and Dr. Fager were the talk of the racing world, and each was a leading contender for Horse of the Year honors.

Ogden Phipps' Buckpasser, champion two-year-old colt of 1965 and champion three-year-old and Horse of the Year of 1966, had won a series of impressive races for older horses while carrying high weights during his four-year-old season. Though plagued by a quarter crack in one of his hooves, the son of Tom Fool and Busanda had won the San Fernando Stakes in January; the Metropolitan Handicap, under 130 pounds, in May after a four-month layoff; and the Suburban Handicap, under 133 pounds, in July in an unforgettable come-from-behind performance. Buckpasser then had lost the July 22 Brooklyn Handicap under a staggering impost of 136, conceding twenty pounds to winner Handsome Boy, to conclude his summer campaign.

Braulio Baeza, who was Buckpasser's regular rider, had replaced Manuel Ycaza as Dr. Fager's rider, beginning with the Arlington Classic, putting Baeza in the enviable position of being the regular rider for two Horse of the Year candidates. Since the Phippses had first call for Baeza to ride Buckpasser, another jockey would have to be found for Dr. Fager in a race against Buckpasser.

For a time it appeared Damascus would get his shot at Buckpasser first, since both colts were nominated for the September 4 Aqueduct Stakes. Buckpasser's trainer Eddie Neloy confirmed he was planning to run the colt in the Aqueduct. New York Racing Association racing secretary Tommy Trotter assigned Buckpasser top weight of 134 pounds with the younger Damascus getting in at 125 pounds. To prepare Buckpasser for the race, Neloy ran him against stablemate Great Power in a public workout on August 29 between races. "(Buckpasser) hears the crowd, sees another horse. It's like a race for him," said Neloy, and Buckpasser responded accordingly. Ridden by Baeza and carrying

134 pounds, the champion colt awed the crowd by making a powerful run at Great Power as the duo turned for home. He soared past his stablemate at the sixteenth pole to clock six furlongs in an impressive 1:10 2/5.

Other horses scheduled for the Aqueduct included the leading older mare Straight Deal; Widener Handicap winner Ring Twice; the speedy Great Power, winner of the Delaware Valley Handicap; and Grey Lag Handicap winner Moontrip. Anticipation for a confrontation between Damascus and Buckpasser built up over Labor Day weekend, but fans were ultimately disappointed. Neloy discovered heat in Buckpasser's right forefoot, the same foot in which he had a quarter crack. Subsequently, Neloy announced that Buckpasser was unlikely to run.

Nevertheless, a crowd of 67,878 showed up for the Aqueduct. Fans were still interested in seeing what the Bancroft colt would do for an encore after his smashing Travers victory and backed him as the solid favorite. As the starting gate opened, Damascus took the lead, but only briefly as Great Power quickly sprinted ahead. At the clubhouse turn Great Power opened a two-length lead over Ring Twice, who raced a half-length ahead of Damascus. Down the backstretch Great Power continued to lead but began dropping back around the far turn. Ring Twice took the lead in the stretch, followed closely by Damascus, with Straight Deal making a strong bid on the outside. Damascus made his patented move to draw clear under mild urging by Shoemaker to win by two lengths. Ring Twice held off a fast-closing Straight Deal by a half-length for second.

After Damascus' victory in the Aqueduct, Whiteley circled the Woodward, the race in which he anticipated meeting Buckpasser and Dr. Fager, for his charge's next engagement.

With Buckpasser's foot mended and Dr. Fager decisively winning the New Hampshire Sweepstakes on September 2, it looked like the Big Three would meet in the mile and a quarter Woodward. The press called it "The Race of the Year for the Horse of the Year," and, in some circles, "The Race of the Century." The Woodward was a weight-for-age event, which meant that three-year-olds would carry a scale weight of 120 pounds while four-year-olds and up would carry 126 pounds. Under handicap conditions Buckpasser might well have ended up with the weight he was assigned for the Aqueduct Stakes, 134 pounds, and be required to give two brilliant colts actual weight.

As the Woodward approached, horse people debated the merits of each colt. The week before the race the *Morning Telegraph* published what some had to say. Elliott Burch, trainer of Sword Dancer, and Carl Hanford, trainer of Kelso, were among those supporting Damascus.

Burch stated: "This is the kind of race where it is almost impossible to make a selection without being in the barns of the major contenders to see how they are coming up to the event. The 3-year-olds are usually better at this time of year than the older horses, as they are consistently improving and the older runners are tailing off a bit. On that basis, I have a slight preference for Damascus, though I must confess some prejudice, as he is by Sword Dancer. At a mile and a quarter, I think he is a better horse than Dr. Fager, though I am not sure."

Commented Hanford: "It is a tremendous task to try to separate this field. I am leaning a bit towards

Damascus right now. Buckpasser, while he has been working well, still hasn't raced since July 22 and that could hurt him. Damascus, on the other hand, has been racing in peak form and he certainly looks fine...The fact that Buckpasser has worked between races with two stablemates at Aqueduct should help him. That's almost like being in competition. He certainly appears to be in great shape. Right now, though, I'd have to say Damascus, on condition and form."

Instead of the "Big Three," some columnists talked about the "Big Four," including Handsome Boy as a contender. The four-year-old colt by Beau Gar out of Marullah showed his ability throughout the year, winning the Nassau County Stakes and the Amory L. Haskell, Washington Park, and Brooklyn handicaps. His most celebrated race was the last-named, in which he defeated the mighty Buckpasser by eight lengths (albeit with that twenty-pound weight differential). Handsome Boy was owned by Hobeau Farm and trained by Allen Jerkens, who had become known as the "Giant Killer." Jerkens had already knocked off Kelso three times with Beau Purple, also a Hobeau Farm-owned son of Beau Gar. In 1973 the trainer would send out Onion to take down the great Secretariat in the Whitney at Saratoga, and in 1998 would defeat eventual Horse of the Year Skip Away with Wagon Limit in the Jockey Club Gold Cup.

In addition to the stars, two other horses were entered in the race, and they generated heated debate among horse people and writers alike. Great Power and Hedevar had been entered by their respective trainers, Neloy and Whiteley, as presumed "rabbits" for Buckpasser and Damascus. "Rabbits" were used in certain circumstances to prompt a fast pace and aid a closing stablemate. Buckpasser had run in previous races with a stablemate that was entered to ensure an honest pace. Interestingly, Buckpasser's stablemate in the Bowling Green, Poker, relished that race's grass course and led all the way to win instead of his illustrious entry-mate.

Damascus did not usually run with a pacesetting entry-mate, though. Since Dr. Fager, with his all-out running style, would be directly affected by the addition of these two horses, Nerud spoke out against the addition of "rabbits." He told Charles Hatton: "You know this is not going to be just a three-horse race. I understand Buckpasser is going to have a sprinter in with him and Damascus could have Hedevar. I seriously doubt if either would care to meet Dr. Fager in a two- or even three-horse race."

Neloy responded in the *Morning Telegraph*: "We're not training Nerud's horses and he's not training ours. I have said before that if you can go into a fight with two guns, it's better than having just one."

Ogden Mills "Dinny" Phipps added: "We are just doing what Nerud did when he sent a pacemaker along with Gallant Man to run against Bold Ruler in the Belmont."

Hatton analyzed the situation for the *Morning Telegraph*: "There are those who infer from Nerud's somewhat apprehensive views that he has a certain lack of confidence in Dr. Fager's ability to emulate such fliers as Count Fleet and War Admiral who never worried about how many white rabbits ran at them."

Whiteley denied he was using Hedevar to help Damascus. "Hell, Hedevar is no rabbit, or whatever they're calling him," and reminded reporters that Hedevar was once co-holder of the world-record mile.

On the day of the race, September 30, Buckpasser

was installed as the favorite, followed by second choices Damascus and Dr. Fager, who were about even in the betting and had the same odds on the tote board. Since Baeza was riding Buckpasser, Bill Boland got the call on Dr. Fager. More than 55,000 fans showed up to root for their favorite in the race, which was also widely broadcast.

The horses went to the post in good order and the official starters released the field: "The Race of the Year for the Horse of the Year" had begun. Hedevar and Great Power, under urging and whipping from their riders, Ron Turcotte and Bob Ussery, respectively, leaped first out of the gate, but by the first turn Dr. Fager had assumed the lead. After the opening quarter in :22 2/5, Great Power dropped out, leaving Hedevar to run with Dr. Fager. Handsome Boy was six lengths back, followed by stretch runners Damascus and Buckpasser. Dr. Fager and Hedevar blazed through the half-mile in :45 1/5 and six furlongs in 1:09 1/5. Down the backstretch Hedevar was through, and Dr. Fager pulled away.

In a sweeping move at the head of the stretch, Damascus came up alongside Dr. Fager. Shoemaker

Damascus was known for his ability to swoop down on his opponents and pass them in the blink of an eye. Jockeys compared his acceleration to stepping on the gas pedal of a big car and zooming away.

Damascus' sire Sword Dancer (top), 1959 Horse of the Year, shared his sire Sunglow's flashy look (above). The two stallions were important in continuing the Teddy sire line. Damascus' dam, Kerala (right, with her 1967 Royal Vale filly), was by the imported My Babu (below), whom Damascus more closely resembled.

Damascus was foaled and raised at John A. Bell III's Jonabell Farm (below with Bell in inset) near Lexington, Kentucky. Damascus' owner Edith Bancroft (above right) boarded her mares at Jonabell for many years. After Edith developed Alzheimer's, her husband Thomas Bancroft Sr. (above with, from left, sons Thomas Jr. and William) and mother, Elsie Woodward (left with Thomas Jr.), managed the family's racing interests.

Trainer Frank Whiteley Jr., who later trained Ruffian and Forego, considered Damascus the greatest horse he had ever been around. Jockey Bill Shoemaker (left with Whiteley) had a special rapport with Damascus, riding the colt to some of his biggest victories. Other jockeys to ride Damascus included Ron Turcotte (above), Manuel Ycaza (top), and Braulio Baeza (above left).

As a two-year-old, Damascus won three of four races, including the Remsen Stakes (top). He got off to a quick start on the Triple Crown trail, winning the Bay Shore Stakes (above) but finished second to Dr. Fager in the Gotham, their first encounter. Damascus returned to romp in the Wood Memorial (right) in his final Kentucky Derby prep.

In the Derby (top), a rank Damascus (in lead on rail) couldn't fend off the late-closing Proud Clarion (far outside) and finished third. The Preakness was another matter. Soothed by the calming influence of his equine pal Duffy (left), Damascus rolled to an easy victory (above left) in the Maryland classic. Damascus' connections — from left, Bancroft Sr., Whiteley, Mrs. Woodward, and Shoemaker — gathered for the trophy presentation.

Damascus captured the Belmont Stakes next (above) to join Native Dancer and Nashua in the ranks of horses that lost the Derby but won the final two legs of the Triple Crown. Mrs. Woodward's late husband William Woodward Sr. had bred Nashua and raced him at three, so the Belmont winner's circle (above right) was familiar territory for her.

During the summer of 1967, Damascus became increasingly dominant, romping in the Leonard Richards Stakes (bottom), Dwyer (left), and American Derby (below).

In the Travers (above), Damascus turned in a devastating twenty-two-length victory and returned to a muddy Saratoga winner's circle (above right). He followed that triumph with another easy win in the Aqueduct Handicap (below).

Hailed by many racing journalists and fans as "The Race of the Century," the 1967 Woodward pitted Damascus against Dr. Fager and Buckpasser, but at the finish, it was all Damascus (below and opposite, inset). Damascus closed out his sophomore season with a victory in the Jockey Club Gold Cup (above) and a narrow loss to Fort Marcy in the Washington, D.C., International. Named Horse of the Year, Damascus paraded for the crowd at Laurel Park that November (opposite, top).

Damascus could be a handful during training hours, kicking up his heels from time to time, but calmly cool out after a work or race.

Damascus began his four-year-old campaign in California, winning the Malibu (right) and San Fernando (above) stakes. Returned to the East Coast, he lost the Suburban to Dr. Fager but later evened the score with a victory over his rival in the Brooklyn Handicap (below).

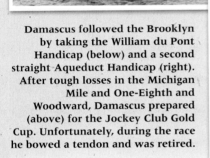

Damascus followed the Brooklyn by taking the William du Pont Handicap (below) and a second straight Aqueduct Handicap (right). After tough losses in the Michigan Mile and One-Eighth and Woodward, Damascus prepared (above) for the Jockey Club Gold Cup. Unfortunately, during the race he bowed a tendon and was retired.

Damascus became a top-notch sire and broodmare sire. Among his outstanding offspring are Honorable Miss (top), Highland Blade (above with the Bancroft brothers), Private Account (above left), Bailjumper (below left), and Timeless Moment (below).

Damascus stood his entire stud career at the Hancock family's Claiborne Farm. Pensioned in 1989, he lived out his days at the Kentucky farm. He died in 1995 and is buried in the farm's Marchmont cemetery.

went to the whip, and Damascus pulled away from Dr. Fager, who was faltering from his early exertions. Buckpasser began his run at the leaders, but Damascus found another gear and steadily widened his lead until he hit the finish line ten lengths ahead of Buckpasser and Dr. Fager. Handsome Boy, not showing his usual flair, finished fourth, thirteen lengths behind Dr. Fager. The final time for the ten furlongs was 2:00 3/5, very close to Kelso's stakes record of 2:00 and Gun Bow's track record of 1:59 3/5.

After the race Shoemaker said, "He's light on his feet, he's got good balance, that horse (Damascus). He's as quick as a cat. I've always been kind of high on him. I hate to praise a horse too much...but in his case, he's improving in all his races. I guess he's as good a horse as I ever rode."

Shortly after the Woodward, Buckpasser, who had already been syndicated for a hefty $4.8 million, was retired to stud at Claiborne Farm. Nerud started Dr. Fager twice more that year, in the October 21 Hawthorne Gold Cup at a mile and a quarter and in the November 7 Vosburgh Handicap at seven furlongs, both of which the colt won easily. Nerud planned to bring the strapping Rough'n Tumble colt back to the races in 1968.

Damascus' victory in the Woodward all but assured his 1967 Horse of the Year mantle. However, debate continued over whether the outcome of the race would have been different without the alleged rabbits present. Damascus' riders Turcotte and Shoemaker maintained that the colt did not need Hedevar to win the Woodward.

In analyzing the Woodward, David Alexander and Charles Hatton wrote that Damascus would have won with or without a rabbit, though they speculated that the margin of victory might have been smaller. Nerud and the Dr. Fager camp disagreed, and their fans and supporters in the press contended that the presence of "rabbits" did make a difference in the outcome of the race.

However, those who observed the Woodward on that autumn day will never forget the sight of three racing legends competing in the same race nor the sight of the bay colt Damascus running all by himself down the stretch. Frank Whiteley will always remember that day and stated for *Racing in America, 1960–1979*:

"I got more kick out of that (the Woodward) than any other race I ever did win."

CHAPTER 8

Accolades And The Campaign Continues

Damascus had won acclaim for his Woodward triumph, but he had two more races ahead as a three-year-old. First, there would be the Jockey Club Gold Cup, a marathon two-mile race that tested its contestants' endurance, and next, the Washington, D.C., International, Damascus' first race on a grass course. Regarding the International, Whiteley told the press, "He's never been on it (the grass), but I can't think of any reason why he shouldn't go good...That would be his last start of the year, I guess."

The October 28 Gold Cup attracted a small but select field of four. Opposing Damascus were the talented Handsome Boy; Successor, who had made a comeback of sorts, winning the Lawrence Realization; and Gentleman James. The two-mile event boasted among its previous winners Buckpasser, Kelso (a five-time winner), Sword Dancer, Gallant Man, Nashua, Citation, and Man o' War. Damascus, Successor, and Gentleman James, under weight-for-age conditions, carried 119 pounds, and the older colt Handsome Boy carried 124.

Handsome Boy took the lead as Shoemaker kept a rank Damascus under firm restraint as the small field passed the stands for the first time. Shoemaker was able to drop Damascus in behind the leader through the clubhouse turn, and his colt finally settled down. Successor followed the top two, and Gentleman James trailed. Down the backstretch, Damascus stalked Handsome Boy, gradually gaining on him.

"It was a slow pace and on the backstretch we could have taken the lead any time, but we waited," observed Shoemaker. "I set him down at the head of the stretch and hit him about four times because he has a tendency to loaf. If we'd had a faster pace he might have broken the record." Shoemaker let Damascus go at the quarter pole, and they easily overtook Handsome Boy, pulling away to win by four and a half lengths in 3:20 1/5. Successor was seven and a half lengths back in third.

Handsome Boy's jockey Angel Cordero Jr. remarked, "...I don't think there's a horse around who can give away weight to Damascus right now."

The Washington, D.C., International, run at one and a half miles, marked Damascus' grass debut and was the only time he faced a field filled with top international racehorses. Run at Laurel Race Course, the November 11 event showcased the American turf specialist Fort Marcy, owned by Paul Mellon's Rokeby Stable, as well as foreign representatives Ribocco, winner of the Irish Sweeps Derby; Speed Symboli, a multiple stakes winner in Japan; the French filly Casaque Grise, winner of the Prix Vermeille; Australian star Tobin Bronze; He's a Smoothie, the colt who became 1967's Canadian Horse of the Year; the South American representative Chateaubriand; and the English stakes-winning filly In Command II. Despite making his first grass start, Damascus was favored.

Whiteley set about preparing Damascus for the race and told William C. Phillips of the *Morning Telegraph*, "The first time I had him on the grass was right after the Woodward. He breezed a couple of times — looked good, too — and galloped a couple of times. He's been either working or galloping on the course here just about every day since we arrived (at Laurel)."

Shoemaker was confident about Damascus' chances. "I don't see why he can't handle grass; he's handled every other kind of track," he said.

As the International got under way, the American contingent of Fort Marcy and Damascus ran just off the pace set by He's a Smoothie, who was followed by Speed Symboli. Heading into the first turn, Fort Marcy overtook the two leaders as Shoemaker moved Damascus past Speed Symboli into third. Leaving the backstretch, Damascus passed He's a Smoothie and came up to Fort Marcy but did not sweep by him as expected. The two raced as a team down the homestretch. Fort Marcy's jockey Manuel Ycaza told Edward L. Bowen of *The Blood-Horse*, "When Damascus came to me at the eighth pole, I still had a fresh horse. We were head and head for a few strides, but I never thought he passed me." The two crossed the wire together, with Fort Marcy getting the decision by a nose in a dramatic photo finish. Tobin Bronze finished third. The final time was 2:27 on a firm course.

As Charles Hatton summed up in the *American Racing Manual*, "Fort Marcy won the money that day, but Damascus won the crowd's heart."

Whiteley later analyzed the International's outcome. "He (Damascus) ran good on the grass...Shoemaker made a couple of moves in there with him. Of course, it was one and a half miles and it was a big field. He ran to that horse again and Fort Marcy beat him by a nose. Damascus was the kind of horse you couldn't drive away from a horse if you ran him to the other horse and gave him a breather. He had to blow by him (the other horse), when he went to him and keep going."

The gelding Fort Marcy would go on to fame and glory as a multiple champion grass horse and as 1970 co-Horse of the Year (with Personality), earning induction into the Racing Hall of Fame in 1998.

Damascus completed his three-year-old season in sensational style, winning twelve of sixteen starts and setting a single season earnings record of $817,941. His hard work was duly rewarded with Horse of the Year honors and a championship for three-year-old colt. A *Morning Telegraph* and *Daily Racing Form* poll also awarded him a handicap championship. In an additional honor, Kenneth Noe, compiler of the *Morning Telegraph* and *Daily Racing Form's* Free Handicap, assigned Damascus top weight of 136 pounds for three-year-olds of 1967, six pounds superior to Dr. Fager.

Damascus' dam, Kerala, also reaped the benefits of her son's success and was named Kentucky Broodmare of the Year and, in addition, because the Bancrofts had a farm in Virginia, the Howell E. Jackson Broodmare of the Year for that state. Quite an honor for a mare that sold for $9,600 as a yearling!

Damascus would have to wait until mid-February of 1968 to get a rest, for Whiteley planned to run him in three stakes races at Santa Anita: the Malibu, San Fernando, and the Charles H. Strub in January and February. He shipped the colt west in December of 1967. Buckpasser had followed the same California race series when he started his four-year-old campaign.

The January 6 Malibu Stakes was run at seven furlongs, a distance Damascus had not contested for nearly a year. A few days before the race, Whiteley gave Damascus a three-furlong blowout work, and the colt completed the move in a sizzling :34 3/5. Even though Santa Anita had a rule against stable ponies accompanying horses to the saddling area, track officials granted permission for Duffy to meet Damascus in the walking ring. "Duffy has become almost as famous as

Damascus, and we wouldn't think of shipping any-where without him," said Bancroft Sr.

Damascus made easy work of the Malibu, and Shoemaker stated, "He's a competitor and the more competition he has, the better he likes it. I shook him up when he got to the lead because he wanted to wait and revive the race." Damascus bested 1967 Santa Anita Derby winner Ruken and 1967 San Felipe Handicap victor Rising Market while carrying high weight of 126 pounds.

Whiteley told the *Morning Telegraph*, "Well, he beat the sprinters at their own game, didn't he?"

Damascus again carried top weight of 126 pounds for the second race in the series, the San Fernando Stakes, at a mile and one-eighth. Unfortunately for Damascus, track officials were not as accommodating of Duffy as they had been for the Malibu but allowed Duffy to accompany Damascus until the horses reached the track.

Soon after the break Field Master, a stakes winner at Golden Gate Fields the previous year, went to the front with Damascus rating in second place. Shoemaker moved Damascus to the lead at the three-eighths pole but had to smack his mount inside the three-sixteenths pole because the colt was gawking and pricking his ears. "Then he jumped tracks near the eighth pole, and I hit him again," said Shoemaker, "but he still wasn't paying attention to me so I got after him again, and then he came on and finished pretty good." "Pretty good" was a two-length victory in 1:48 4/5.

The San Fernando ended up being Shoemaker's final race on Damascus. Three days later the jockey broke the femur of his right leg in a race at Santa Anita when his mount Bel Bush took a serious spill. The extent of the injury and the treatment would keep Shoemaker from riding for more than a year. Whiteley told the *Washington Post* later that year: "That injury (Shoemaker's) hurt us," and explained, "Shoemaker knew the horse and fit him well. Damascus was the easiest horse to ride, if you knew him. I never gave Shoemaker an order on him, and he got the job done nearly all the time." To this day Whiteley stresses how important Shoemaker was to the career of his champion colt and commented in 2002, "(Shoemaker) made a big difference to Damascus."

Shoemaker would go on to ride many other racing

greats, including Forego and Spectacular Bid, but recalled of Damascus, "I think he'd run all day. He was a really top, top horse, and he should have been a Triple Crown winner. He never got his full due as far as I'm concerned. He was a great horse."

Whiteley contacted Ron Turcotte, who had pinch hit for the team the previous year, to ride Damascus in the one and a quarter-mile Strub Stakes, which at $118,700-added was the richest race in the series. The race was taking place a little later in February than normal because of a horsemen's boycott and subsequent stoppage of racing at Santa Anita. Damascus, at odds of 1-5, faced five other horses that included Most Host, Ruken, and Proud Land. Rain the day before had left the track slow.

Perhaps he didn't relish the going or displayed his tendency to loaf when running next to Most Host or, as some writers speculated, missed Shoemaker, but Damascus struggled against a lesser rival. At the quarter-pole Damascus put a head in front of Most Host, but his opponent was not finished. The two raced down the stretch as a team. As they hit the wire, Most Host had his head in front and scored an upset, paying $26.40 to win in a relatively slow 2:04.

After the race Most Host's jockey, William Harmatz, commented to reporters, "Beating Damascus is just one of those things you can't believe. It won't sink in. Truthfully, all I was hoping for was second money. To win it is like a dream."

Turcotte in 2002 revisited the Strub: "Ruken and Damascus didn't have mud shoes on that day. Damascus was…slipping and sliding all the way but he still finished second. I mean it was an amazing race. I went to the barn after, and he was really cut up all over, right up his shoe; he lost one shoe and the other one turned sideways and cut his leg…

"I wish I could have ridden Damascus all the time," he added, "but Whitney Tower (in *Sports Illustrated*) wrote such a bad story on me (criticizing his ride in the Strub)…They took me off the horse; I never got to ride him again."

Damascus finally got his vacation and was shipped to Camden, South Carolina, to rest and prepare for the challenges ahead.

CHAPTER 9

Damascus Vs. Dr. Fager, Again

After Damascus' rest and relaxation in Camden, Whiteley started his colt back on the road to competition by bringing him to Laurel Race Course. Getting him back into shape was a gradual process. Whiteley reported in late April to the *Morning Telegraph* that for about seven weeks he had been walking the colt for about one and a half to two hours each day, and "...a couple of weeks ago he began to feel his oats, so last week I began to take him to the track for gallops."

Whiteley was impressed with the colt's appearance, convinced Damascus had never looked better. The trainer had his eye on the handicap division but worried about the weight Damascus would have to carry. He, nevertheless, pointed the colt toward the Suburban Handicap and did not rule out other handicaps in the quest for another Horse of the Year title.

Damascus was moved to Delaware Park in late May to prepare for his first race after the layoff. Manuel Ycaza got the assignment for Damascus' return, a June 17 allowance at a mile and seventy yards. Perhaps reacting to the excitement of returning to competition, Damascus was frisky in the paddock and in the post parade. The overmatched field saw only Damascus' heels in the stretch as he raced to an easy three and three-quarters-length victory over pacesetting Light the Fuse.

Ycaza enthusiastically praised the colt: "I've ridden a lot of great horses during my time, but I doubt I was ever on a better one. Yes, I know he didn't beat much, but he has this wonderful action and, when you chirp he takes off, just like you're stepping on the accelerator of a big car. I was amazed by his motion and his response...It was a pleasure to ride Damascus. I've been chasing him so many times that I've often wondered how it would feel to be in the driver's seat. Well, it feels great."

Likewise, Whiteley was pleased with Damascus' race. "Yes, I told Ycaza to let him gallop out. But he was in better shape than I thought. I figured he'd get a little tired, but he came back to the barn kicking and playing as if he hadn't been raced at all. I guess I'd like to get another race in him before he runs in a stakes. As I say, the race yesterday was designed to get him tired, and we didn't achieve our goal, so he may need another."

As it turned out, Damascus would face Dr. Fager in his next race, the mile and a quarter Suburban Handicap on July 4. Named champion sprinter of 1967, the Rough'n Tumble colt had begun his four-year-old campaign with the May 4 Roseben Handicap at Aqueduct under 130 pounds. John L. Rotz, subbing for Braulio Baeza who was riding in the Kentucky Derby, partnered the colt to an easy three-length victory, covering the seven furlongs in 1:21 2/5. John Nerud then shipped Dr. Fager to Hollywood Park for the mile and one-sixteenth Californian Stakes, and the big colt won it just as easily, this time with Baeza up and again carrying 130 pounds.

Nerud announced plans to run Dr. Fager in the Metropolitan Handicap, but a very severe case of colic forced the horse to miss the race. While Dr. Fager was recovering, In Reality took the Metropolitan Handicap over Advocator, covering the mile in a swift 1:35. In

Reality's trainer, "Sunshine" Calvert, informed the media that the Intentionally colt would compete in the next race of the New York Handicap Triple Crown series, the Suburban. With Nerud returning Dr. Fager to training for this race and Whiteley announcing that Damascus would run, the Suburban was shaping up to be the most anticipated race of the year. NYRA racing secretary Tommy Trotter assigned 133 pounds to Damascus, 132 to Dr. Fager, and 125 to In Reality. Other horses announced for the race were Amerigo Lady, Bold Hour, and Hedevar. Dr. Fager was made the even-money favorite, followed by the Damascus-Hedevar entry at 6-5 and In Reality at 5-1.

As it turned out, Hedevar was scratched from the Suburban, thereby changing the race's dynamics. For Damascus' rider, Ycaza, it would be either let Dr. Fager loose on the lead or if the other colt was not challenged by any other horse, go after him, somewhat like being between a rock and a hard place. Some writers, including Joe Hirsch of the *Morning Telegraph*, observed that Damascus "was a trifle high in flesh."

Just out of the starting gate, In Reality took a few bad steps and ran dismally. His connections later discovered he had fractured a cannon bone, an injury which caused his early retirement. Ycaza took Damascus to the lead briefly, but Dr. Fager quickly took over. Baeza let the "Good Doctor" run in relatively slow fractions — :48 2/5 at the half. With In Reality out of it, Ycaza moved Damascus closer to Dr. Fager, who was quite relaxed on the lead. Although, this was an atypical race for Damascus, this tactic would hopefully prevent Dr. Fager from getting loose on the lead and stealing the race. As they moved around the turn, Dr. Fager was slightly ahead with Damascus bearing down on him; the two raced together, picking up the pace to zip the third quarter in :22 3/5. As they pounded down the stretch, the slower early fractions and the weight began to take their toll on Damascus. Dr. Fager began to open up his lead, with Bold Hour, carrying seventeen pounds less than Damascus, in hot pursuit. At the finish line Dr. Fager was ahead by two lengths, followed by Bold Hour, with Damascus another three lengths back in third. The final time of 1:59 3/5 for the one and a quarter miles equaled the track record at Aqueduct.

After the race John Nerud told Charles Hatton, "I

told Baeza to go slow as he could in front of them, and he said, 'that depends what the pace is like.' Damascus broke on top but Ycaza did not insist. In the backstretch, he realized what was going on and that Baeza had gone a half in about :48. He (Ycaza) did the only thing he could do."

Despite that strenuous and challenging effort, Damascus returned to the races for the July 13 Amory L. Haskell Handicap at Monmouth Park, carrying top weight, this time 131 pounds. He again faced Bold Hour, who was getting another big break in the weights at 116 pounds, and Mr. Right, who was carrying 114 pounds. Whiteley indicated to reporter Joe Hirsch that perhaps a rematch with Dr. Fager in the July 20 Brooklyn Handicap might be in Damascus' future provided Damascus came out of the Haskell in good shape. "We want another shot at that horse," Whiteley added. "It would mean three hard races for Damascus in three weeks, but I believe he can handle it. Besides, there is really no important engagement for our horse after the Brooklyn until the Aqueduct on Labor Day."

In the Haskell the rapidly improving Bold Hour

made the most of the break in the weights. Damascus stumbled as the gates opened, but Ycaza hung on and tried to get his mount in gear. King's Palace took the lead, followed by Ninfalo and Bold Hour. Damascus raced toward the back of the pack into the backstretch. At the quarter-pole Bold Hour moved alongside King's Palace and took the lead as they headed into the stretch, with Damascus moving up on the outside, followed by Mr. Right. Damascus got to within a length of Bold Hour but lacked the necessary punch to get by his rival. Bold Hour then pulled away with authority to defeat Mr. Right, who outdid Damascus at the wire. The final time was 2:03 for the mile and a quarter.

Former Calumet Farm trainer H.A. "Jimmy" Jones, then director of racing at Monmouth Park, noted that Damascus' stumble from the gate cost him. "Often this sort of thing knocks a horse out of gear for the remainder of the trip and that's about what occurred. He went into the first turn with dirt flying in his face and he was climbing as if he were out of sorts," Jones told the *Morning Telegraph*. "Then, after they had 'trotted' a half-mile in :48, he was about eight lengths off the lead, which isn't what you want when you've got to come so far out of it. There's no wonder he tended to hang after making that big move. He almost got to the lead...And, too, when a horse is carrying more than 130 pounds, it is often virtually impossible for him to overcome impending situations and still win. I'd say Damascus ran a big race under the circumstances."

After two setbacks in a row, Damascus was shipped to Aqueduct for his fourth confrontation with Dr. Fager, this time in the mile and a quarter Brooklyn Handicap. As a result of Dr. Fager's Suburban triumph, Trotter assigned the colt 135 to Damascus' 130. Hedevar would be Damascus' running mate. Despite his weight disadvantage and the presence of the free-running Hedevar, Dr. Fager was still installed as the favorite. Many fans, horsemen, and media thought that Dr. Fager was more formidable at four, able to conserve his awesome speed in the early stages of the race, with or without a pacesetter present.

Hedevar and his jockey, Tommy Lee, broke in front and had three lengths on Dr. Fager into the first turn. Damascus was held off the pace behind Mr. Right and Advocator. Along the backstretch Dr. Fager started after Hedevar. Lee later reported to *The Blood-Horse* that he slowed the pace with Hedevar so Dr. Fager "would come on and run past me, which he did at about the three-quarters marker." After a half-mile, run in :45 4/5, Dr. Fager was in the lead while Damascus still trailed but was running easily. Approaching the far turn, Damascus made his run and quickly closed on his rival, who was about to clock a mile in 1:34 3/5. Damascus pulled away in the stretch to win by two and a half lengths over Dr. Fager, who was flipping his tail, clearly resenting Baeza's use of the whip to urge him on. As it turned out, Damascus would have the distinction of being the only horse to finish ahead of Dr. Fager in 1968. Damascus set a still-standing track record of 1:59 1/5 in the Brooklyn.

"(Damascus) could scarcely have finished faster were he dropped off the roof," wrote Charles Hatton in the 1969 *American Racing Manual*.

Whiteley acknowledged that Damascus got a little help from Hedevar. "He's (Damascus) a one-run horse — when the race is run his way. If the pace is slow, of course, he can give you more than that. It was run his way today," he told *The Blood-Horse*. Damascus' connections had an extra reason to celebrate the colt's

Brooklyn win since it made him the eighth equine millionaire, with earnings of $1,025,526.

William H. Rudy in his *Racing in America, 1960–1979* would later write: "To some extent (Damascus) needed a race to be run his way—but so did Dr. Fager."

Spectators at Aqueduct had the added drama of three jockeys who participated in the Brooklyn boarding a helicopter in the infield to take them to Monmouth Park. The helicopter, owned by Mrs. H.C. Phipps, carried Manuel Ycaza, Braulio Baeza, and John L. Rotz to Monmouth Park, where they would ride in the Sorority Stakes. The Brooklyn marked the last meeting of the titans, but even in only four races Damascus and Dr. Fager had forged a memorable rivalry, ending up two and two, that would be etched in the memories of their fans and provoke debate for decades to come.

After the Brooklyn Handicap, Damascus still had plenty more to do, and Whiteley told reporters that after giving Damascus a brief rest, the Sword Dancer colt would return to the races later that summer.

CHAPTER 10

Triumph And Defeat

E ventually, his grueling racing schedule, increasingly heavy imposts, and an injury would take their toll on the durable Damascus. But his four-year-old season continued unabated in the August 10 William du Pont Jr. Handicap at Delaware Park. Damascus' regular rider, Manuel Ycaza, had been riding the great filly Dark Mirage to her victories, including the New York triple crown for fillies, and he had committed to ride her in the Alabama Stakes at Saratoga. An injury would keep Dark Mirage from running in that race, but Braulio Baeza, Dr. Fager's regular rider, already had been assigned to ride Damascus. The William du Pont Jr. Handicap would mark the colt's heaviest assignment, for he would be carrying a hefty 134 pounds.

Regardless of the weight, Damascus was installed as

the 1-5 favorite over competition that included stakes winners Big Rock Candy, Fast Count, and Charles Elliott. At the start Big Rock Candy took the lead and set a relatively slow pace. Baeza noted, "After a quarter I realized that the pace was very slow, so I let out a notch and allowed him to roll along. I didn't want them to get too far away under these conditions. Once asked for speed he responded smartly and was simply too much for his field." Damascus pulled away from his opponents and won by two lengths over Big Rock Candy and Charles Elliott, running the one and one-sixteenth miles in 1:43 3/5. Baeza described Damascus as a "nice easy horse to ride."

Whiteley shipped Damascus to New York for the Aqueduct Stakes, a race his colt had won very easily in 1967. He faced Ring Twice, runner-up in the 1967 Aqueduct; More Scents, a multiple stakes winner whose victories included the Bernard Baruch Handicap; Out of the Way, the three-year-old stakes winner whose triumphs included the Jersey Derby; and the stakes winners Fort Drum and Spoon Bait. Damascus carried 134 pounds, and this time gave away from thirteen to twenty pounds to his rivals, a more challenging group than he had faced at Delaware. Again faced with a slow pace, Baeza moved Damascus a little closer to the leaders to keep them within his sights. "When we straightened out in the stretch and I asked him for his run — he had it," the jockey recalled. Damascus made easy work of the assignment, winning by one and a half lengths in hand over More Scents with Fort Drum in third.

Whiteley next shipped Damascus to Detroit Race Course for the September 14 Michigan Mile and One-Eighth. Damascus would again be required to carry highweight, this time 133 pounds, and spot his rivals from fifteen to twenty-four pounds. Baeza was again aboard Damascus; Turcotte would ride Hedevar, who would get in with 112 pounds. A field of twelve showed up. Rivals described by the *Morning Telegraph* as having upset potential were Nodouble, an up-and-coming three-year-old who had won that year's Arkansas Derby, and Stanislas, who had upset Tom Rolfe to win the 1966 Michigan Mile and One-Eighth.

Hedevar and Misty Run set much of the pace, with Nodouble just off them in third. Damascus settled back in tenth. In the backstretch Nodouble moved up on the leaders, and Hedevar started to drop back. Around the stretch turn Nodouble and Misty Run battled for the lead. With less than three-eighths of a mile left, Damascus was gaining, but it was too late; Nodouble was too far ahead. Damascus shot by Misty Run but did not catch Nodouble, who finished two and three-quarters lengths ahead. The final time was 1:49.

Whiteley thought Baeza had waited too long to make his move. But Baeza disagreed. "He did not accelerate like he normally did," the jockey recalled. "Something was bothering the horse; he was not the same horse."

In the years after the race, Nodouble, a son of Noholme II, would become a handicap star in his own right, with victories including the 1969 Santa Anita Handicap, Californian Stakes, and Brooklyn Handicap, and he would earn champion older horse honors in 1969 and 1970.

The 1968 Woodward Stakes, run on September 28 at the newly refurbished Belmont Park, would not have the drama and excitement of the previous year's showdown among champions. After the Brooklyn Handicap, Damascus' rival Dr. Fager completed a sensational summer, adding to his string of victories with an eight-length win in the Whitney Handicap and a world-record mile of 1:32 1/5 posted in the Washington Park Handicap. John Nerud indicated that Dr. Fager would not run in the Woodward Stakes but instead on the grass in the September 11 United Nations Handicap, which Dr. Fager subsequently won. It now appeared that Damascus and Dr. Fager would not face each other again — much to the disappointment of their fans.

Damascus, carrying scale weight of 126 pounds in the mile and a quarter Woodward, would face other — equally weighted — horses: Mr. Right, Grace Born, and Fort Drum. There was much pressure on Damascus to win this race if he wanted to stay in the hunt for year-end honors. His defeat in Detroit had been a major setback, and some of the press and horsemen now considered Dr. Fager to be the leading contender for Horse of the Year.

Fans installed Damascus as the overwhelming favorite. The outcome would disappoint Damascus' supporters and create controversy. Grace Born took the lead with Damascus following uncharacteristically

LEGENDS

close. William H. Rudy commented for *The Blood-Horse*, "It has been Damascus' history that when he contests the lead, as he did in the Suburban with Dr. Fager, he fails to win." Once Damascus disposed of Grace Born, Mr. Right moved in for the challenge. The pair dueled the rest of the way. Rudy commented that at the finish, "Damascus appeared to fight back once more, missing by the dropping of a nose in a finish so close that some called him the victor." His fans' collective dissent rang out when Mr. Right's number was placed first. The horse had scored a major upset in a time of 2:03.

Baeza told reporters after the race, "There was no pace and everybody was holding back. I guess that hurt; maybe he hung a little right at the end." Many race goers booed Baeza after he rode out on the track for the next race. Owner Bancroft told the press, "I believe that if (Baeza) had hit him, he would have won it." Whiteley, in turn, announced that Baeza would be replaced as regular rider of Damascus. "Everyone knows my horse does not like to race the way he did in the Woodward. I don't know why Baeza did it, and I didn't ask him." Whiteley expressed his dissatisfaction with Baeza's ride later in 1968 to the *Washington Post*:

"Take the Woodward Stakes...If you would have wanted Damascus to get beat, you would have ridden him exactly the same way Baeza did that day. I told him to let Mr. Right and the others go, but he came out of the gate hustling on the horse...Damascus was the kind of horse who would rate in behind a two-minute clip if not stirred up early. Shoemaker learned early on Damascus that it was wise to keep him relaxed as much as possible."

Baeza maintained that Damascus was hurting that day and therefore not himself. Turcotte, who rode Damascus and competed against him on many occasions, said in 2002, "Damascus was a very sore horse when Baeza rode him...He wasn't right when Nodouble beat him in the Michigan Mile...He wasn't right when Mr. Right beat him...I was the regular rider for Mr. Right. He was not that caliber of horse at all. (Heliodoro) Gustines rode Mr. Right that day...Damascus was no way close to himself (in the Woodward)."

Whiteley announced that Damascus' next three starts would be the Man o' War, Jockey Club Gold Cup, and the Washington, D.C., International. Since two of the three races would be on the grass, Damascus spent many of his workouts on the Belmont turf course. Damascus appeared to relish his turf workouts, but his enthusiasm got the better of him. The colt apparently "rapped" himself on a foreleg and injured an area near a tendon. Whiteley described the injury as "touch and go" for a while, but Damascus mended.

Damascus continued his training, but Whiteley changed the colt's schedule to make the October 26 Jockey Club Gold Cup his last race. Ycaza, who last rode Damascus to probably his most successful race of the year, the Brooklyn Handicap, was chosen to partner him in the Gold Cup. The week before the race, rumors swirled that the colt was "off." William H. Rudy of *The Blood-Horse* wrote, "(Damascus) had not been to the track, it was said. He had broken down. He was doubtful for the two-mile Cup Race…"

The weather that day was cold, cloudy, and gloomy, but more than 40,000 fans turned out for the race, in which Damascus would face Mr. Right; the good handicap horse Quicken Tree; Funny Fellow; Chompion; and Draft Card. To race goers' surprise, track announcer Fred Caposella announced a jockey change for

Damascus: Larry Adams would replace Ycaza, who had strained a back muscle and was taking the rest of the day off. When Damascus entered the Belmont paddock, he was wearing tendon bandages in front for the first time. Apparently, bettors were cautious about Damascus' chances, failing to make him the odds-on choice for one of the few times in his career. The chestnut gelding Quicken Tree was the second betting choice.

Damascus settled into his usual position off the pace. Then, to the dismay of the crowd, Damascus dropped back more than thirty lengths behind the leader, Quicken Tree. Past the wire he appeared to stumble, and Larry Adams dismounted. The crowd was riveted on the ailing Damascus, instead of Quicken Tree, who was returning to the winner's circle. A horse ambulance came to collect Damascus, who appeared very uncomfortable, gingerly stepping into the ambulance. Comments like "the poor horse" and "why did they race him today?" resonated throughout the crowd. Larry Adams told reporters, "He walked to the gate perfectly, and I thought he warmed up well. He was full of run coming out of the gate and was fighting me the first time through the stretch. That's why I took him off the rail. I wanted him to relax a little. I wanted to make a big move coming to the three-eighths pole. When I got there, I clucked to him and let him out and really expected to roll, but he didn't have a thing."

Veterinarian William O. Reed took little time to diagnose Damascus with a bowed tendon in the same foreleg the colt had injured while training. Reed put Damascus' left foreleg in a cast and to relieve the colt's discomfort, injected his shoulder with a painkiller. Reed told William Rudy of *The Blood-Horse*, "No rupture of the tendon, and right now it appears there's no bone involvement. He's been the soundest horse on the race track...He was like a piece of steel this morning. He was sound this morning."

The Monday after the Gold Cup, Thomas Bancroft announced Damascus' retirement. "Actually, it is not a terribly bad bow, and it will not interfere with his starting stud duty next February," he said.

Damascus retired with twenty-one victories in thirty-two starts and career earnings of $1,176,781, placing him sixth on the list of all-time leading money-winning Thoroughbreds. It took a career-ending injury to force him to finish out of the money for the first and only time, such was his consistency.

Damascus was vanned from Belmont to Laurel Race Course, where he would recuperate. On November 2, the same day old rival Dr. Fager clinched Horse of the Year honors with a commanding Vosburgh victory, Turf writer Teddy Cox visited Frank Whiteley and Damascus at Laurel to see how the colt was progressing. Damascus at this stage was not frolicsome or playful but behaved as if he knew the danger of aggravating the injury. Whiteley observed: "When a horse is at his physical peak, there is danger that he will injure himself if he doesn't get sufficient exercise. In this colt's case the danger would be greater if not for his perfect disposition and intelligence."

Whiteley looked back on the day of the Jockey Club Gold Cup and acknowledged he had seriously considered scratching Damascus after Ycaza canceled his mounts for the day. "Something told me that this was not his day. I wasn't really certain about his condition but had reasons to believe he was fit enough," said the trainer. "I didn't think he'd ever be put under pressure to beat such an ordinary field going that day. Usually, such a race is merely a long, slow gallop and they are not subjected to the type of raw speed that breaks down horses...He came up for the race apparently in fine shape, and the leg he hurt had not shown any signs of inflammation or heat."

Whiteley refuted the rumors that he was "forced" by Bancroft to run the Sword Dancer colt: "Absolutely not! Naturally, I talked it over with Mr. Bancroft. For a time it was touch and go whether running him would be feasible. But I made the final decision after I felt reasonably certain that the horse was physically fit and would run a good race."

For Damascus, it was the end of a brilliant and remarkable racing career but the beginning of his stallion career, during which he would have the opportunity to pass on his greatness and durability to new generations.

CHAPTER 11

Saving The Teddy Line

W hile Damascus recuperated at Laurel Race Course, his syndication was underway. A number of groups in Virginia and Kentucky expressed interest in standing Damascus, as did some Europeans. Bancroft's goal was to ensure that Damascus be bred to the best mares. Damascus was an especially prized stallion prospect, not only because of his sterling achievements as a racehorse but because he would be bequeathing the Teddy line to his offspring.

Not surprisingly, A.B. Hancock Jr., owner of Claiborne Farm, wanted to stand Damascus and won out over other suitors. The Bancrofts retained six shares, and the remaining twenty-six were sold for $80,000 each, giving Damascus a total value of $2.56 million.

Damascus joined select company at Claiborne Farm, home at the time to leading sires Bold Ruler, Round

Table, Tulyar, Ambiorix, Double Jay, and champions Buckpasser, Tom Rolfe, and Forli.

Syndicate members represented the highest echelon of owners and breeders, among them Paul Mellon, James Cox Brady, John W. Galbreath, Robert Kleberg Jr., Mrs. Martha Gerry, Walter Salmon Jr., and T.M. Evans.

Damascus arrived at Claiborne on December 5, 1968. In his first season he was bred to thirty-eight mares, among them stakes winners Come Hither Look, Jet to Market, Desert Love, Trade Mark, Lady Brilliance, Swift Lady, Spearfish, and Paris Pike. Stakes producers booked to Damascus included the dams of Hedevar, Lamb Chop, King's Bishop, Farewell Party, and Twice Cited.

Breeders speculated that Damascus would succeed at stud and surpass his sire Sword Dancer. Sword Dancer sired just fifteen stakes winners and eventually ended up in Venezuela. Pedigree expert Leon Rasmussen analyzed Damascus' chances for sire success in the *Thoroughbred Record*: "If the Teddy line is to survive in the classic perspective, it could well be up to Damascus, a superior race horse who was honest and durable as well as full of quality."

Disposition-wise, Damascus was, according to Claiborne Farm manager Gus Koch, "a very easy horse to work with. We never had any problems with him."

Damascus' first foals, born in 1970, were an intriguing and diverse group that attracted notice from the start. Honorable Miss out of the Bancrofts' mare Court Circuit was his first winner; she inherited Court Circuit's lop-eared look and was a spirited filly who raced against the males at sprint distances, usually coming from off the pace in a dramatic finish. Affectionately dubbed "Old Lop Ears" by some of the press, she won the Fall Highweight Handicap twice. A tough campaigner, she raced until the age of six and compiled career earnings of $437,973. Whiteley recalled that of all the Damascus offspring he trained, Honorable Miss was the best. Honorable Miss was thought so highly of that she had a stakes race at Saratoga named after her. Unfortunately, not one of her offspring showed the same talent as a racehorse.

Timeless Moment, out of the Native Dancer mare Hour of Parting, resembled his paternal grandsire, Sword Dancer, and was Damascus' first stakes winner.

Specializing in shorter races, Timeless Moment's most memorable performance was the 1974 Nassau County Handicap, in which he defeated the great Forego. Damascus was also represented in his first crop by stakes winner Crown the Prince, stakes-placed winners Penny Flight and Damascene, and good allowance winner Cutlass.

It was apparent from the performers in his early crops that Damascus was off to an excellent start, and breeders showed faith in him by sending the best mares, among them Numbered Account, Shuvee, Politely, Desert Vixen, and Moccasin, as well as the dams of champions Arts and Letters, Bold Bidder, Reviewer, Queen of the Stage, Ruffian, and Dahlia. Damascus' offspring came in all varieties and some inherited their sire's unique amber eyes. Some also inherited his head-down running style, their necks and tails a straight line when they were fully extended. Koch noted that the colts tended to be more amenable to training while the fillies were on the feisty side. "The Damascus fillies were strong-willed and would try to fight you every step of the way," he recalled.

As the years went by, Damascus was represented by

a number of first-class performers: Lord Durham, the 1973 champion two-year-old in Canada; Belted Earl (out of Moccasin), the 1982 champion older horse and sprinter in Ireland; Damascus Regal, the 1988 champion older horse in Italy; and stakes winners that included Soy Numero Uno, Highland Blade, Crusader Sword, Judger, Sarsar, Regal Rumor, Time for a Change, Eastern Echo, Private Account, Celine, Bailjumper, Confidential Talk, and Ogygian. Among Damascus' sons to place in the classics were Diabolo, Highland Blade, and Desert Wine. Damascus' offspring ran at all distances, some excelling at sprint races, some specializing in races of a mile and a quarter or more.

Many of Damascus' sons excelled as sires, and the ones that were most influential in carrying on the Teddy male line were Private Account, Bailjumper, Time for a Change, Timeless Moment, Cutlass, and Eastern Echo.

Private Account, a foal of 1976, was one of Damascus' most royally bred offspring, being out of Buckpasser's champion daughter Numbered Account. Private Account was also one of his sire's nicest-looking foals, inheriting his parents' best features. Bred by

Ogden Phipps, Private Account won impressively at three and four and was termed "the genuine article" by newspaper handicappers. He won the Jim Dandy Stakes at three and Gulfstream Park and Widener handicaps at four, earning $339,396. Whiteley thought Private Account was the best of all Damascus' offspring to race. However, Private Account's greatest impact has been as a sire.

Joining Damascus at Claiborne Farm, Private Account became an immensely successful stallion and his 1984 filly out of Grecian Banner, Personal Ensign, became a racing legend, the first major modern racehorse to retire undefeated. Personal Ensign has also achieved success as a broodmare, producing stakes winners Miner's Mark, Traditionally, and My Flag and stakes-placed Our Emblem and Proud and True. She was named Broodmare of the Year in 1996. The year 2002 was significant for Personal Ensign: her son, Our Emblem, sired Derby-Preakness winner War Emblem, and she became maternal granddam (through My Flag) of 2002 champion two-year-old filly Storm Flag Flying. Personal Ensign has built her own dynasty: she won the Breeders' Cup Distaff in 1988, her daughter

My Flag won the Breeders' Cup Juvenile Fillies in 1995, and her granddaughter Storm Flag Flying won the Breeders' Cup Juvenile Fillies in 2002, a unique feat in Breeders' Cup history. Private Account also sired champion filly Inside Information, Personal Flag, Secret Hello, Private Terms, Corporate Report, and Classy Cathy. Personal Flag, Personal Ensign's full brother, sired the popular Say Florida Sandy, who became the first New York-bred to earn more than two-million dollars. Private Account is a successful leading broodmare sire as well. Fertility problems prematurely ended Private Account's career as a stallion in 1995. He is now a pensioner at Claiborne Farm, where many of his descendants also reside. In 2003 Gus Koch reported that the pensioner still "looks great."

Bailjumper, Court Circuit's 1974 Damascus colt, had lopped ears like his sister Honorable Miss. He won at longer distances than she, including the mile and one-eighth Dwyer and the one-mile Saranac. He retired to stud at Jonabell Farm, where he was foaled. His best son was Skip Trial, a 1982 colt from Looks Promising, by Promised Land. Looks Promising descended in her male line from Sun Again, thus giving Skip Trial an additional cross to the Teddy line. Skip Trial became a multiple stakes winner of $1,837,451 whose victories included the Haskell Invitational, Pegasus Handicap, Pennsylvania Derby, Gulfstream Park Handicap (twice), and Massachusetts Handicap. Skip Trial's most-accomplished son is Skip Away, a 1993 foal out of Diplomat Way's daughter Ingot Way. Skip Away won stakes races across America, winning honors as best three-year-old of 1996, best older horse of 1997, and Horse of the Year of 1998. He retired as the second-leading money-winning Thoroughbred of all time with earnings of $9,616,360. His victories included the Jockey Club Gold Cup (twice), Woodward Stakes, Breeders' Cup Classic, Massachusetts Handicap, Gulfstream Park Handicap, Pimlico Special, and Hollywood Gold Cup. His unique "Stairmaster" stride and his durability attracted many fans across the country. His first crop included graded stakes-placed Christmas Away, a foal of 2000.

In addition to Skip Trial, Bailjumper's other stakes winners included the filly Cappucino Bay. She went on to produce a colt by El Prado, named Medaglia d'Oro, who in 2002 and 2003 racked up several major stakes wins, including the Travers, Jim Dandy, Whitney, and Strub Stakes.

Time for a Change, Damascus' 1981 son out of Resolver, upset champion Devil's Bag in the 1984 Flamingo Stakes. The lightly raced Time for a Change missed the classics due to health problems and an injury forced his retirement at age four. Time for a Change, chestnut like his grandsire, sired Fly So Free, who was named 1990 champion two-year-old colt. Fly So Free became a successful sire, and among his offspring are 1999 Canadian champion turf mare Free Vacation and 2001 Dubai World Cup winner Captain Steve.

The aforementioned Timeless Moment sired the handsome chestnut Gilded Time. His best son to race, Gilded Time was named 1992 champion two-year-old colt. An injury kept Gilded Time from the Triple Crown races, but he had immediate success at stud, becoming the nation's leading first crop sire in 1997. Gilded Time has consistently produced useful performers and was represented in 2002 and 2003 by the outstanding filly Mandy's Gold. Interestingly, Mandy's Gold won the Honorable Miss Stakes in 2002.

Also mentioned earlier, Cutlass, a son of the Dunce

mare Aphonia, became an outstanding sire in Florida, siring forty stakes winners including handicap star Cutlass Reality, Friendly Lover, Boys Nite Out, Chaldea, and Puerto Rican champion Fight for U P. R. Additionally, Cutlass sired the dam of promising stakes-winning 2003 juvenile colt, Chapel Royal.

Eastern Echo, a foal of 1988 out of Northern Dancer's daughter Wild Applause, won the Futurity at two and was a promising racehorse whose career was cut short by an injury. Successful as a stallion, he was represented by stakes winners that included Swiss Yodeler and Buddy Gil. The latter, a gelding, made headlines as he won major three-year-old races on the West Coast in preparation for the 2003 classics. Swiss Yodeler not only did well at the racetrack, winning major stakes such as the Hollywood Futurity and Hollywood Juvenile Championship, but was an immediate success as a stallion, becoming the leading sire of two-year-olds in California and among the leading sires of two-year-olds on a national level.

Damascus excelled as a broodmare sire, with his daughters producing more than 150 stakes winners, including champions Chilukki, Proskona, Dictator's

Song, Someday Jack, Black Beauty D., Taldari, and El Sultan. Among Damascus' other stakes winners as a broodmare sire are Coronado's Quest, Desert Stormer, Marlin, Capades, Boundary, Splendid Spruce, Dixieland Heat, and Shadeed. In addition, the leading sire Red Ransom, whose promising racing career was curtailed by injury, was by Roberto from Damascus' daughter Arabia; the champion grass mare Perfect Sting has been Red Ransom's best performer. Another Damascus daughter, Sword Game, when bred to Secretariat produced Sister Dot, who became the dam of champion two-year-old and popular young sire Dehere. Dixieland Heat, by Dixieland Band out of the Damascus mare Evening Silk, is a successful sire, numbering among his offspring the champion filly Xtra Heat.

Damascus' career as a sire flourished. He eventually produced seventy-one stakes winners and was consistently among the leading sires and broodmare sires. He did well with mares from all sire lines, but many of his stakes winners came from mares from the sire lines of Bold Ruler, Buckpasser, Ribot, Turn-to, and Northern Dancer.

The Teddy line, once thought dormant, is once

again alive and thriving through Damascus, his sons, grandsons, and great-grandsons. His daughters also keep his name prominent in the pedigrees of today's outstanding racehorses and leading sires.

DAMASCUS

EPILOGUE

Senior Statesman

In 1989, at age twenty-five, Damascus was pensioned from stud duty due to declining fertility. For the next six years Damascus and 1968 English Horse of the Year Sir Ivor were the official "senior statesmen" at Claiborne Farm. Damascus was genetically disposed toward longevity, evidenced by Sword Dancer, who lived until the age of twenty-eight, and by Kerala, who died at twenty-six. Still, time was catching up with the distinguished Claiborne stallions. Sir Ivor passed away in early 1995, and the infirmities of old age were increasingly afflicting Damascus. Cataracts clouded his amber eyes, and his back legs were weakening; his once glossy coat had become dull.

Claiborne groom Tommy Walton had looked after Damascus for many years and had the bittersweet duty of caring for him as the elderly champion's condition deteriorated. On August 8, 1995, Damascus died while sleeping in his paddock. He was buried in the Marchmont cemetery at Claiborne, next to fellow Hall of Famer Easy Goer. He had outlived his rivals from decades past: Buckpasser, Dr. Fager, and In Reality.

As of 2003, at Claiborne Farm, Damascus descendants Boundary, Out of Place, Private Terms, and Coronado's Quest stood there at stud. The last-named stallion, who was very spirited on the racetrack, has settled down and is now a "perfect gentleman," according to Gus Koch.

After the deaths of Thomas Bancroft Sr. in 1970 and Edith Bancroft the following year, their sons Thomas Jr. and William continued the stable, this time under the name Pen-Y-Bryn Farm — the same name as their late parents' farm in Virginia. Elsie Cryder Woodward lived to see the success of her grandsons' Pen-Y-Bryn Farm; she passed away in 1981 at the age of ninety-eight. Called by the *New York Times* "one of the last grande dames of New York society," Mrs. Woodward died in her sleep at her long-time residence at the Waldorf Towers.

Both Frank Whiteley and his son David trained for

the Bancroft sons. Even after his retirement in 1984, Frank Whiteley, who was inducted into the Racing Hall of Fame in 1978, still prepared the Bancrofts' two-year-olds for the races in Camden, South Carolina, and sent them to the racetracks, where David trained them.

The descendants of the original foundation mares purchased by Edith Bancroft and Elsie Woodward in the late fifties comprised the horses raced by the Bancrofts over the years, including Highland Blade (from the Penny Bryn family), Zen (Penny Bryn), Stiff Sentence (Cycle), Instrument Landing (Creme Brulee), Cloudy Dawn (Creme Brulee), Bailjumper (Cycle), Cyamome (Creme Brulee), and Honorable Miss (Cycle).

Kerala, one of these foundation mares, did not produce another Damascus, though Sword Dancer would sire two more of her offspring: an unnamed colt of 1969 that died in a fire at Jonabell Farm in 1970 and Arlene Francis, a 1970 filly who won some races but was, according to Frank Whiteley, "just a horse." Arlene Francis, a namesake of Mrs. Woodward's actress friend, did produce a stakes winner in Fabulous Find for Pen-Y-Bryn Farm. Kerala's name appeared in the pedigree of 2002 Wood Memorial winner Buddha; he is descended through his dam from Beaufix, Kerala's daughter by Weather Bureau. Kerala later produced sons and daughters sired by the fashionable stallions Nijinsky II, Bold Reason, Majestic Prince, Tom Rolfe, and Arts and Letters, but none approached the greatness of Damascus. Kerala died in 1984 and is buried at Jonabell Farm, where she spent almost her entire life. Sword Dancer, Damascus' sire, also died in 1984, in Venezuela, where he achieved some success as a broodmare sire. In addition to Damascus, Sword Dancer was represented by one other champion, Lady Pitt.

In 1995 the Bancrofts ceased operation of Pen-Y-Bryn Farm, having sold off their racing and breeding stock and shares in stallions. As of 2003, the famous white and red-dotted silks are inactive.

In 1974, six years after Damascus retired, Frank Whiteley took on the training of the immortal filly Ruffian, arguably the greatest racing filly of all time. The almost-coal-black filly was champion at two and three but tragically broke a leg in the infamous match race with 1975 Kentucky Derby winner Foolish Pleasure at Belmont Park and had to be euthanized. Whiteley went on to train the mighty Forego, taking over from Sherrill Ward in 1976 and 1977. One of the greatest geldings and handicap stars of all time, the tall and strong Forego carried heavy weights and beat the best horses of his era. He was Horse of the Year from 1974 to 1976 and champion older horse in 1977. Damascus, Ruffian, and Forego are all members of the Racing Hall of Fame.

But for Frank Whiteley, Damascus was extra special. He paid tribute to the champion: "I'll tell you this much, there'll never be another like him. He was truly the greatest horse I've ever been around."

DAMASCUS'
PEDIGREE

		Sun Again, 1939	Sun Teddy Hug Again
	Sunglow, 1947		
		Rosern, 1927	Mad Hatter Rosedrop
SWORD DANCER, ch, 1956			
		By Jimminy, 1941	Pharamond II Buginarug
	Highland Fling, 1950		
		Swing Time, 1935	Royal Minstrel Speed Boat
DAMASCUS, bay colt, 1964			
		Djebel, 1937	Tourbillon Loika
	My Babu, 1945		
		Perfume II, 1938	Badruddin Lavendula
KERALA, b, 1958			
		Sickle, 1924	Phalaris Selene
	Blade of Time, 1938		
		Bar Nothing, 1933	Blue Larkspur Beaming Beauty

DAMASCUS' RACE RECORD

Damascus **b. c. 1964, by Sword Dancer (Sunglow)–Kerala, by My Babu** **Lifetime record: 32 21 7 3 $1,176,781**

Own.– Mrs Edith W. Bancroft
Br.– Mrs Thomas Bancroft (Ky)
Tr.– F.Y. Whiteley Jr

26Oct68- 7Bel	gd 2	:50^{2} 2:31^{3} 3:22^{4}	3↑	J C Gold Cup 109k	1	3	4^{8}	6^{12}	6^{24}	6^{37}	Adams L	124	*1.30	48-16	QuickenTree124^{1¼}FunnyFllow119^{3½}Chmpon119^{3}	Bowed tendon	6
28Sep68- 7Bel	fst 1¼	:47^{2} 1:11^{3} 1:37 2:03	3↑	Woodward 106k	3	2	1^{hd}	1^{hd}	1^{hd}	2no	Baeza B	126	*.10	85-16	Mr. Right126^{no}Damascus126^{7}Grace Born126^{16}	Just failed	4
14Sep68- 9Det	fst 1⅛	:47^{1} 1:11^{1} 1:36^{1} 1:49	3↑	Mich 1⅛ H 123k	1	9	10^{14}	7^{9½}	6^{6¾}	2^{2¾}	Baeza B	133	*.30e	93-19	Nodouble111^{2¾}Dmscs133^{hd}MstyRun109^{2¼}	Very wide stretch	12
2Sep68- 7Aqu	fst 1⅛	:47 1:11 1:35^{4} 1:48^{2}	3↑	Aqueduct 108k	4	3	3^{5}	3^{3}	2^{½}	1^{1½}	Baeza B	134	*.40	94-13	Damascus134^{1½}More Scents114^{8}Fort Drum114^{3}	Going away	6
10Aug68- 8Del	fst $1\frac{1}{16}$	:24 :48^{4} 1:12^{3} 1:43^{3}	3↑	W Du Pont H 53k	4	5	3^{1}	2^{hd}	1^{hd}	1^{2}	Baeza B	134	*.20	91-20	Damascus134^{2}BigRockCandy113^{¾}CharlesElliott110^{10}	Driving	5
20Jly68- 7Aqu	fst 1¼	:45^{4} 1:09^{2} 1:34^{3} 1:59^{1}	3↑	Brooklyn H 109k	2	5	5^{11}	2^{½}	1^{½}	1^{2½}	Ycaza M	130	1.40e	102-13	Damascus130^{2½}Dr. Fager135^{3}Mr. Right114^{hd}	Won going away	7
13Jly68- 8Mth	fst 1¼	:48 1:12^{1} 1:37^{1} 2:03	3↑	AL Haskell H 111k	6	6	6^{8}	3^{3}	2^{1}	3^{1½}	Ycaza M	131	*.60	85-16	BoldHour116^{1¼}Mr.Rght114^{nk}Dmscus131^{5}	Stumbled after start	8
4Jly68- 7Aqu	fst 1¼	:48^{2} 1:11 1:34^{3} 1:59^{3}	3↑	Suburban H 107k	1	2	2^{½}	2^{hd}	2^{2}	3^{5}	Ycaza M	133	1.40	95-11	Dr. Fager132^{2}Bold Hour116^{3}Damascus133^{3½}	Failed to rally	5
17Jun68- 5Del	fst 1 70	:23^{4} :47^{3} 1:11^{4} 1:40^{2}	4↑	Alw 10000	3	3	2^{4}	2^{hd}	1^{1}	1^{3¾}	Ycaza M	124	*.10	98-16	Damascus124^{3¾}LighttheFuse119^{6}ClassicWork120^{nk}	Handily	5
10Feb68- 8SA	sl 1¼	:48^{2} 1:13^{1} 1:38^{2} 2:04		C H Strub 118k	1	5	5^{7}	1^{½}	1^{hd}	2^{hd}	Turcotte R	126	*.20	78-22	Most Host114^{hd}Damscs126^{10}Ruken117^{½}	Gave way gradually	6
20Jan68- 6SA	fst 1⅛	:49 1:13 1:37^{1} 1:48^{4}		San Fernando 56k	4	2	2^{½}	1^{hd}	1^{1}	1^{2}	Shoemaker W	126	*.10	88-12	Damascs126^{2}Most Host113^{hd}Ruken120^{4½}	Won drawing clear	6
6Jan68- 8SA	fst 7f	:22^{3} :45 1:09 1:21^{1}		Malibu 45k	4	1	3^{2½}	3^{½}	1^{½}	1^{2½}	Shoemaker W	126	*.40	97-15	Damascus126^{2½}Rising Market120^{nk}Ruken123^{1}	Handily	8
11Nov67- 7Lrl	fm 1½Ⓣ	:49^{1} 1:14 2:03 2:27	3↑	D C Int'l 150k	2	4	4^{3½}	3^{½}	2^{hd}	2no	Shoemaker W	120	*.60	84-13	FortMarcy120^{no}Dmascus120^{2½}TobinBronze127^{2½}	Just failed	9
28Oct67- 7Aqu	fst 2	:49^{4} 2:30^{2} 2:55^{4} 3:20^{1}	3↑	J C Gold Cup 106k	1	2	2^{2}	2^{hd}	1^{4}	1^{4½}	Shoemaker W	119	*.30	95-12	Dmascus119^{4½}HandsomBoy124^{7½}Successr119^{6½}	Handy score	4
30Sep67- 7Aqu	fst 1¼	:45^{1} 1:09^{1} 1:35^{3} 2:00^{3}	3↑	Woodward 107k	5	5	5^{12}	1^{½}	1^{5}	1^{10}	Shoemaker W	120	1.80e	95-15	Damascus120^{10}Buckpasser126^{½}Dr. Fager120^{13}	Easy score	6
4Sep67- 7Aqu	fst 1⅛	:48^{2} 1:12^{1} 1:36^{1} 1:48^{1}	3↑	Aqueduct 106k	3	3	3^{4}	3^{2}	1^{hd}	1^{2}	Shoemaker W	125	*.30	95-14	Damascus125^{2}Ring Twice119^{½}Straight Deal116^{6}	Handily	5
19Aug67- 6Sar	sly 1¼	:45^{4} 1:11 1:36^{4} 2:01^{3}		Travers 80k	4	3	3^{16}	1^{6}	1^{10}	1^{22}	Shoemaker W	126	*.20	100-10	Damascus126^{22}Reason to Hail120^{7}Tumiga117^{5}	Won eased up	4
5Aug67- 8AP	fst 1⅛	:46 1:10^{1} 1:34^{3} 1:46^{4}		American Derby 120k	2	6	6^{12}	6^{6¼}	1^{4}	1^{7}	Shoemaker W	126	*.80	101-16	Damascus126^{7}InReality120^{3}FavorableTurn112^{1½}	Ridden out	7
15Jly67- 7Aqu	sly 1¼	:47^{3} 1:12 1:37^{4} 2:03		Dwyer H 83k	6	9	9^{12}	2^{1}	1^{hd}	1^{¾}	Shoemaker W	128	*.50	83-18	Damascus128^{¾}FavorableTurn112^{2½}BlastingChrg116^{hd}	Driving	9
8Jly67- 8Del	fst $1\frac{1}{16}$	:23^{4} :47^{1} 1:10^{4} 1:42^{1}	3↑	W Du Pont Jr H 54k	4	5	5^{8}	4^{3}	2^{1}	2no	Shoemaker W	121	*.20	98-12	Exceedingly113^{no}Damascus121^{4}Flag Raiser114^{5}	Hung	5
17Jun67- 8Del	fst 1⅛	:47 1:11^{3} 1:37 1:49^{1}		Leonard Richards 41k	4	4	3^{2½}	1^{½}	1^{hd}	1^{3¼}	Turcotte R	126	*.10	91-13	Damascus126^{3¼}Misty Cloud119^{1½}Favorable Turn119^{2½}	Easily	6
3Jun67- 8Aqu	fst 1½	:47 1:12^{2} 2:02^{3} 2:28^{4}		Belmont 148k	1	6	5^{9½}	3^{1}	2^{hd}	1^{2½}	Shoemaker W	126	*.80	87-15	Dmascus126^{2½}CoolReception126^{½}GentlmanJams126^{1}	In hand	9
20May67- 8Pim	fst $1\frac{3}{16}$	:46^{2} 1:10^{4} 1:36^{4} 1:55^{1}		Preakness 194k	2	9	8^{11}	8^{6}	1^{3½}	1^{2¼}	Shoemaker W	126	*1.80e	97-11	Damascus126^{2¼}In Reality126^{4}Proud Clarion126^{¾}	Ridden out	10
6May67- 7CD	fst 1¼	:46^{3} 1:10^{4} 1:36 2:00^{3}		Ky Derby 162k	2	6	4^{4}	4^{1½}	3^{2}	3^{4}	Shoemaker W	126	*1.70	93-07	ProudClarion126^{1}BarbsDelight126^{3}Damascus126^{1¼}	Bid,hung	14
22Apr67- 7Aqu	fst 1⅛	:46^{2} 1:10^{4} 1:36^{3} 1:49^{3}		Wood Memorial 112k	4	3	4^{5}	4^{2}	1^{1}	1^{6}	Shoemaker W	126	*.70	88-16	Damascus126^{6}Gala Performance126^{3}Dawn Glory126^{1½}	Easily	9
15Apr67- 7Aqu	fst 1	:23^{3} :46^{1} 1:10^{2} 1:35^{1}		Gotham 57k	9	2	2^{3}	2^{hd}	1^{hd}	2^{½}	Shoemaker W	122	*1.30	91-14	Dr. Fager122^{½}Damascus122^{5}Reason to Hail114^{7}	Game try	9
25Mar67- 7Aqu	my 7f	:22^{4} :46^{4} 1:12^{4} 1:25^{4}		Bay Shore 28k	1	4	4^{6}	4^{5½}	2^{2}	1^{2½}	Shoemaker W	115	2.40	77-35	Damascus115^{2½}Disciplinarian117^{1½}Nhoc'sBullt110^{3}	Driving	7
11Mar67- 7Pim	fst 6f	:23^{3} :47^{2} 1:12^{1}		Alw 5000	8	3	3^{1½}	4^{2}	5^{3¼}	1^{hd}	Shuk N	122	*.60	89-16	Dmascus122^{hd}Solar Bomb122^{1½}Last Cry119^{½}	Bumped late,up	8
30Nov66- 7Aqu	gd 1	:23^{1} :46 1:11^{2} 1:37		Remsen 30k	2	3	2^{hd}	3^{2}	4^{¾}	1^{1½}	Shoemaker W	117	*1.30	83-22	Damascus117^{1½}NativeGuile117^{½}ReflectedGlory119^{¾}	Driving	14
29Oct66- 3Lrl	fst 7f	:22^{4} :46^{2} 1:12^{1} 1:25^{1}		©Alw 4000	2	1	1^{½}	1^{2}	1^{9}	1^{12}	Shoemaker W	119	*.40	93-16	Damascus119^{12}Joxer115^{3½}Roman Away117^{2½}	Scored in hand	7
12Oct66- 5Aqu	fst 7f	:23 :46^{2} 1:12 1:24^{3}		©Md Sp Wt	8	1	1^{1}	1^{1}	1^{4}	1^{8}	Shoemaker W	122	*.90	83-18	Damascus122^{8}Winslow Homer122^{5}Gun Mount122^{1}	Easily	14
28Sep66- 4Aqu	fst 7f	:22^{3} :46 1:11^{3} 1:24^{3}		©Md Sp Wt	11	9	7^{6}	7^{7½}	3^{2½}	2^{2½}	Shoemaker W	122	*2.60	80-19	Comprador122^{2½}Damascus122^{¾}Air Rights122^{1}	Game try	14

Index

151

Photo Credits

Cover photo: (NYRA/Paul Schafer)

Page 1: Damascus with Bill Shoemaker up (Jerry Frutkoff); Damascus winning at Aqueduct (NYRA/Bob Coglianese)

Page 2: Sunglow (Keeneland-Morgan); Sword Dancer (Skeets Meadors); Kerala (Skeets Meadors); My Babu (Skeets Meadors)

Page 3: Elsie Woodward and Tom Bancroft Jr. (Winants Bros.); Edith Bancroft (Keeneland-Morgan); Tom Bancroft Sr. and sons (NYRA/Mike Sirico); John A. Bell III (The Blood-Horse); Jonabell Farm (Skeets Meadors)

Page 4: Frank Whiteley and Bill Shoemaker (The Blood-Horse); Manuel Ycaza up (NYRA/Bob Coglianese); Braulio Baeza up (NYRA/Bob Coglianese); Ron Turcotte up (Ed Ewing)

Page 5: Damascus winning the Remsen (NYRA/Bob Coglianese); Winning the Bay Shore (NYRA/Paul Schafer); Winning the Wood Memorial (NYRA/Bob Coglianese)

Page 6-7: Proud Clarion's Derby (The Blood-Horse); Damascus winning the Preakness (Jacques L. Morin); Damascus and Duffy (The Blood-Horse); Preakness winner's circle (Jerry Frutkoff); Damascus in Belmont winner's circle (NYRA/Mike Sirico); Shoemaker petting Damascus (Winants Bros.); Belmont trophy presentation (Winants Bros.)

Page 8: Damascus winning the Leonard Richards (Ed Ewing); After winning the Dwyer (NYRA/Bob Coglianese); Winning the American Derby (The Blood-Horse)

Page 9: Winning the Travers (The Blood-Horse); Travers winner's circle (the Blood-Horse); Winning the Aqueduct (NYRA/Bob Coglianese)

Page 10-11: Winning the Jockey Club Gold Cup (NYRA/Bob Coglianese); Side view of Woodward win (NYRA/Mike Sirico); Front view of Woodward win (NYRA/Bob Coglianese); Parading at Laurel (Jerry Frutkoff)

Page 12: Damascus galloping at Saratoga (The Blood-Horse); Damascus kicking up his heels (The Blood-Horse); Cooling out (Winants Bros.)

Page 13: Winning the Malibu (The Blood-Horse); Winning the San Fernando (The Blood-Horse); Winning the Brooklyn (NYRA/Mike Sirico)

Page 14: Winning the William du Pont (Ed Ewing); Winning the 1968 Aqueduct (NYRA/Bob Coglianese); Damascus jogging (NYRA/Paul Schafer)

Page 15: Honorable Miss (NYRA/Bob Coglianese); Highland Blade (The Blood-Horse); Private Account (Turfotos); Bailjumper (NYRA/Bob Coglianese); Timeless Moment (Turfotos)

Page 16: Damascus conformation (John Noye); Gravestone (Tom Hall)

Back cover: Remsen winner's circle (Mike Sirico)

ABOUT THE
AUTHOR

L ucy Heckman is an associate professor at St. John's University in Jamaica, New York, head of reference for the school's library, and a freelance writer. She has also written *The New York Stock Exchange: A Guide to Information Sources; The Nasdaq: A Guide to Information Sources;* and *Franchising in Business.*

Damascus is her first book about Thoroughbred racing, a sport in which she has had a lifelong interest. Heckman lives in Queens Village, New York.